A PLAGUE OF PRISONS

A PLAGUE
OF PRISONS

The Epidemiology of
Mass Incarceration in America

Ernest Drucker

THE NEW PRESS

NEW YORK
LONDON

Requests for permission to reproduce selections from this book should be mailed to:
Permissions Department, The New Press, 38 Greene Street, New York, NY 10013.

Published in the United States by The New Press, New York, 2011
Distributed by Perseus Distribution

LIBRARY OF CONGRESS CATALOGING-IN-PUBLICATION DATA
Drucker, Ernest.
    A plague of prisons : the epidemiology of mass incarceration in America /
Ernest Drucker.
        p.   cm.
    Includes bibliographical references and index.
    ISBN 978-1-59558-497-7 (hc. : alk. paper)   1. Imprisonment—United
States.   2. Imprisonment—Social aspects—United States.   3. Criminal
justice, Administration of—Social aspects—United States.   I. Title.
HV8705.D78   2011
365'.975—dc22   2011002072

The New Press was established in 1990 as a not-for-profit alternative to the large,
commercial publishing houses currently dominating the book publishing industry. The
New Press operates in the public interest rather than for private gain, and is committed
to publishing, in innovative ways, works of educational, cultural, and community value
that are often deemed insufficiently profitable.

www.thenewpress.com

Composition by dix! Digital Prepress
This book was set in Minion

Printed in the United States of America

10   9   8   7   6   5   4   3   2

To my father, Joe Drucker,
who taught by example,
bearing life's hard knocks without complaint.
He had the strong mind and focus of an engineer
and a knack for fixing things.
From him I learned
about meeting obligations and the pride and dignity
of those who do their job well.

Thanks, Dad.

CONTENTS

ACKNOWLEDGMENTS

My gratitude to the Soros Foundation and to the Open Society Institute and its Social Justice Fellowship Program, which supported my initial work on this book and so many of my other projects over the years, with special thanks to George Soros, Aryeh Neier, Gara LaMarche, Hamilton Fish, Susan Tucker, and to the other Soros Justice Fellows who provided great inspiration and from whom I learned so much. Thanks to Ethan Nadelmann, who has always led the way. I am also greatly indebted to the National Institutes of Health (NIH) and my project officer Jerry Flanzer for many years of understanding and generous support for my own research; the Fogarty International Program of the NIH and the World Health Organization for early experiences in drug policy and primary care in the UK; and the University of New South Wales School of Community Medicine, Sydney University's Menzies Center for Health Policy, and the Fulbright/Australian Senior Specialist Program in Global Health. For external support, thanks to David Rogers and the Robert Wood Johnson Foundation; amfAR, the Foundation for AIDS Research (particularly Mathilde Krim, who always showed up on the demonstration lines); Phil Lee, who made the right connections; and the JEHT Foundation (fallen to Madoff), which supported the work with Ricardo Barreras at Family Justice/ La Bodega de la Familia. And a special thanks to Robert Field for his generous personal support when I needed it most.

Montefiore Medical Center and its leader, Martin Cherkasky, gave me a home for over forty years and an unequaled source of education, experience, and a sense of purpose that formed the foundation for my career and for much of this book. My thanks to Marianne Kennedy, Sharon Lockett, Bill Wasserman, Alexandra Bobadilla, Kathy Eric, Anitra Pivnick, Sippio Small, Brigette Poust-Mercurio, and Ellen Tuchman for all the hard work at Monte in thirty years of our programs; the social medicine and epidemiology chairs, Vic Sidel and Michael Alderman, for their support; the teams at Spofford Juvenile Center and Rikers Island Health Services who launched my life in prisons, with their visionary leaders in adolescent medicine (Michael Cohen, Iris Litt, and Ken Schoenberg) and in adult prison health (Bobbie Cohen, Bob Greifinger, Eran Bellin, and Steve Safyer); and my old friend Dorothy Levinson, who showed me the way from the Bronx to Australia.

I'm especially grateful for the many years of political and intellectual sustenance from my comrades in the drug policy reform movement—first, Ethan Nadelmann at the Drug Policy Foundation, the Lindesmith Center, and now the Drug Policy Alliance. Also thanks to Pat O'Hare and the global harm-reduction movement that grew into the International Harm Reduction Association, shaping the framework for so many of the ideas about drugs and public health presented in this book. From a cast of hundreds, I applaud Arnold Trebach, Kevin Zeese, Harry Levine, John Morgan, Lynn Zimmer, Loren Seigel, Ira Glasser, Craig Reinermann, Dan Waldorf, Marsha Rosenbaum, Sheigla Murphy, Gabriel Sayegh, Dave Purchase, Allan Clear, Edith Springer, Andrew Tatarsky, Dan Bigg, Sharon Stancliff, Jennifer McNeely, Bruce Trigg, Joey Tranchina, Les Pappas, Hindi Bernstein, Holly Catania, and the Reverend Howard Moody (to name just a few), plus Dr. Alvarez de Choudens (Don Papo), Dr. Carmen Albizu, and Dr. Salvador Santiago and their families, working so long and so hard at drug law reform in Puerto Rico.

My appreciation and admiration to the great Australians who thought in terms of public health models of drugs from the outset and successfully held AIDS back for thirty years, teaching the lesson that a whole society could get these policies right (mostly).

Cheers for Alex Wodak, Ingrid van Beek, Lisa Maher, David Dixon, Kate Dolan and Margaret McDonald, Dave Burrows, Andrew Byrne, Nick Crofts, Jimmy Dorabjee, Michael Moore, and for the friendship and support of Gavin Frost, Steve Leeder, and Beverly Fielder. And my warmest thanks for the wonderful political savvy and humane insights of my friends and political comrades Ann Symonds and Michael Kirby.

Helping to build real harm-reduction programs within a health care system in Vancouver was a privilege and an important formative experience for me, as Canada gave birth to landmark initiatives in drug policy, treatment, and HIV prevention. All were guided by another set of gifted and effective public health professionals and political leaders: Dan Small, David Marsh, Evan Wood, Thomas Kerr, Perry Kendall, Gillian Maxwell, Donald MacPherson, and Philip Owen, who led a succession of Vancouver mayors who got it right, building on the earlier work of Eugene Oscapella, Diane Riley, Pat Erickson, and Eric Single in Ontario. In the UK, where I got my start thinking differently about drugs in the 1960s, thanks to Frankie Armstrong, Brian Pearson, John Booth Davies, and again Pat O'Hare and all the Liverpool pioneers on harm reduction. There were many supporters of harm reduction in Europe: in Germany, Ilya Michaels, Hans Haengeline, and Hans Jaeger; in Switzerland, Robert Haemmig and Ambrose Uchtenhagen; in France, Bernard Kouchner, Bertrand LeBeau, and Patrick Aeberhard; and of course the Dutch, Jean-Paul Grund, Mario Lap, Peter Cohen, and Freek Pollack—plus Fabio Mesquita in Brazil and southeast Asia. And my thoughts are still with some of our fallen American heroes of harm reduction: Rod Sorge, John Waters, and Keith Cylar.

In criminal justice I found a world of great thinkers, activists, and teachers: Nils Christie in Oslo, JoAnne Page and Glenn Martin at the Fortune Society, Liz Gaines at the Osborne Association, Bob Gangi at the New York Correctional Association, and Jamie Fellner at Human Right Watch, and Wilbert Rideau and Norris Henderson in New Orleans. At John Jay College of Criminal Justice, I discovered a hotbed of new ideas about criminal justice and new colleagues who quickly became old friends, thanks to Ric Curtis: Bilal Khan, Anthony Marcus, Travis Wendel, Kirk Dombrowski, Martin Horn, Doug Tompkins, and Evan Mandery. John Jay gave me a new academic home late in my career thanks to Ben Rohdin, Jane Bowers, and Jeremy Travis. I also wish to thank all the brilliant and dedicated people I found in the world of criminal justice services and advocacy: Robin Steinberg and MacGregor Smyth at Bronx Defenders; Eric Cadora at the Justice Mapping Center; Jim Parsons at the Vera Institute; Tulia defense attorneys Jeff Blackburn and Vanita Gupta; Albany prosecutor David Soares; researchers Judy Greene, Marc Mauer, and Christopher Wildeman; Christina Hoven and the Stress and Justice research team at Columbia; and Corrine Cary at the NYCLU. Max Kenner, Jed Tucker, and Daniel Karpowitz of the Bard Prison Initiative put me back in prison— to teach, that is—and they and the students created a whole new chapter in my understanding of the limitations and possibilities of prison education. I have deep respect and affection for that diverse crowd of committed activists who made things happen on the ground and paid the bills in Tulia and Great Barrington: Randy Credico, Judy Knight, Ben Hillman, David Scribner, Peter Greer, and Steve Picheny, to name a few.

My friends and colleagues in AIDS and public health helped me earn my stripes in the sort of interdisciplinary social epidemiology that this book represents: Peter Selwyn, Jerry Friedland, Sten Vermund, Preston Marx, Bill Schneider, Laurie Garrett, and Stephen Flynn. My special thanks goes to my friend and colleague Ricardo Barreras, who worked closely with me on many of the formative projects in social network research presented in the book.

My gratitude for all the great teachers from the public school system of New York City, which offered me a PhD for the price of the subway rides: Martin Starfield at Brooklyn Tech; Larry Plotkin, Kenneth Clark, and Daniel Lehrman at City College of New York;

and my clinical and public health mentors and colleagues, Angel Fiasche at Maimonides Community Mental Health Center; Fred Schwartz at the Austen Riggs Center in Stockbridge; Martin Cherkasky, Vic Sidel, and Roberto Belmar at Montefiore Medical Center/Albert Einstein College of Medicine; Allan Rosenfield, Alan Berkman, and the Family Susser at Columbia's Mailman School of Public Health; and Alfred Gellhorn, Pyser Edelsack, and Jack Geiger at the City College Medical School.

For my own "deep sources," I am indebted to the inspiring personal and intellectual support of a few great friends and mentors in the biomedical sciences, social justice, ethics, public health history, and human rights: Jonathan Mann, Robert Newman, Anthony Mazzochi, Vincent Dole, Renee Fox, Robert Sweet, and Michael Kirby; to the many younger peers, colleagues, and co-workers who became valued friends over the decades: Peter Lurie, David Michaels, Les Pappas, Alan Ross and Nellie Corea, Richard Horton, Helena Hanson, Richard Elovich, Homer Venters, and Dahlia Heller and Savanna Reid; and to the group of fine students from whom I learned much and who helped substantively with my own research: Jacob Hupart, Josie Valentine, Mindy Brittner, Michelle Cornacchia, Myles Dickason, Marc Pimental, and Pattie O'Brien for her great skill and creativity illustrating many of my charts and graphs.

My eternal gratitude to The New Press and its editorial director Diane Wachtell, whose understanding of the book's new paradigm and this new way of telling an old story made this book possible. Diane guided me at every step of the way and without her this book wouldn't exist. Also my great thanks for so much help from Tara Grove, Sarah Fan, and all the others at Greene Street.

Also my great thanks for early support by friends: Peter Press and his parents, Larry and Sally; Gillian Walker, Albert Maysles, and their kids; and Dick Mayo-Smith and Tom Roderick at Educators for Social Responsibility. Kudos to Anthony Nordoff, who made my garden grow so I could write in peace, and Steve Berkowitz

DDS and Dr. Jenny Lin, Dr. Ira Nash, and Dr. Nicolas Skipitaris at Mount Sinai and Nestor Cabanillas in Buenos Aires, who help keep my engine running well past 100,000 miles.

Saving the best for last, my love and appreciation for all her years of support to my dearest friend and wife, Jeri—for our entire life together; to Jesse Drucker and Nell Casey, both seasoned writers full of encouragement and sound advice for a new author and parents of our family jewels, Hank and Eve; and to fellow grandparent and writing pro Jane Barnes. Thanks to my brother Alan and sister-in-law Jayne; Kenny Drucker, Leslie Berger, Jacob, Nathan, and Bella; and Elaine and Henry Jeria for all their warmth and good cheer; plus the elders Herby Drucker, Henry J. Rosner, and that centurian force Ruth Gruber, who kept after me to complete this book and warned me not to wander too far from the storyline. God bless you all.

1

AN EPIDEMIOLOGICAL RIDDLE

An "unusual event" has occurred in which a great loss of life has taken place. The population involved in the event was large and very diverse: men and women, adults and children, different social classes—the rich, the middle class, and the poor. Can we use the available data—a few details about who lived and who died—along with some tools of epidemiology (the science of public health) to figure out what that "unusual event" was? Here are the things we know:

- Over two-thirds of the more than two thousand people involved died.
- Among the adult population, women were three times as likely to survive as men.
- The children under twelve years of age were almost 50 percent more likely to survive than the adults.
- Those in the highest social class were 50 percent more likely to survive than the middle class, and over twice as likely to survive as the lower class.

What was the event? A lethal new virus? An act of terrorism or war? A natural disaster? An accident? How can this sparse "mortality data" on the differences between those who survived and those who perished point the way to the solution?

Epidemiologists use tables to organize data systematically in a way that reflects details about all the individuals exposed to an event (or disease), sorted out by who died and who survived. The two outcomes, life and death, can be categorized and cross-referenced by gender, age, and economic status to give a portrait of how each one affects an individual's odds of death or survival, and how these three variables interact with each other.

Figure 1.1 gives us the basic mortality data from this event expressed as rates. Of the 2,224 people involved in our unusual event, 1,513, or 68 percent, died, and 711, or 32 percent (fewer than one in three), survived. The actual number of deaths can be deceptive—it's the rates that matter: the proportion who survived and its inverse, the proportion who died.

What do we know from this first piece of evidence that can help us solve the puzzle? First off, 68 percent—what epidemiologists call the overall or crude mortality rate—is a very high proportion of deaths for any disease or disaster. For an idea of what this

Figure 1.1. Social and Demographic Characteristics of the Population at Risk and Death Rates for Each Subgroup

	Number and Percent of Population at Risk	Number and Percent of Deaths in Each Group
Men	1,690 (76%)	1,352 (80%)
Women	425 (19%)	109 (26%)
Children (under 12 years)	109 (5%)	52 (48%)
TOTAL	2,224 (100%)	Total Deaths = 1,513 (68%)
Upper Social Class	325 (15%)	122 (38%)
Middle Social Class	285 (13%)	167 (59%)
Lower Social Class	706 (32%)	528 (75%)
Social class data not available	908 (41%)	696 (77%)
TOTAL	2,224 (100%)	Total Deaths = 1,513 (68%)

While more than two-thirds of all the 2,224 people at risk died, the death rates for each of the subgroups differs dramatically: 80 percent of the men died, but only 26 percent of the women and 48 percent of the children. Social class was a powerful predictor of death: among the upper class, 38 percent died (i.e., two-thirds survived), but in the lower class, 75 percent died. The 908 people for whom social class data was unavailable seem to follow the pattern of the lower social class with the highest death rate of all, 77 percent.

Source: Population and Mortality Data from Official Commission Investigating the Event.

death rate signifies, recall that over 2,800 people died in the World Trade Center attack of 9/11, but about 10,000 were in the buildings when the planes struck. The mortality rate of any event that takes many lives is the number of deaths divided by the number of people exposed—the total number at risk for death. So we can say the entire population in the WTC buildings was at risk at the time the planes struck, and that the 28 percent mortality rate in the WTC attack is the proportion that died among all those who were exposed—less than half the mortality rate of our mystery event.

Was our unusual event a particular outbreak of an epidemic disease? Few long-known diseases kill such a large proportion of those who get infected (e.g., malaria eventually kills about 25 percent, but over many years). But some newer diseases (such as Ebola) kill a much higher proportion; of those who are infected with the Ebola virus, about 90 percent quickly die. So our event could be an outbreak of a new, very lethal virus that struck a village of two thousand people. Or maybe it is some sort of accident—a train or plane crash? Many plane crashes have a 100 percent mortality rate, but in some cases all survive (Sullenberger's remarkable landing in the Hudson River in the winter of 2009, for example). In most plane crashes, many die but, on average, two-thirds survive. However, no plane holds two thousand people, so that's an unlikely answer. But some crowded commuter trains hold more than that. Could it be a huge accident? A terrorist bombing? It could be a wartime battle, where tens of thousands can die, or the tsunami of 2008 in Indonesia, or the Haitian earthquake of 2010 that killed over three hundred thousand—huge numbers with very high death rates similar to those of our event.

But how do we account for the differences in death rate by age, gender, and social class? What disease or disaster would produce this particular pattern of death rates? One of the most common factors affecting health, life expectancy, and the risk for many diseases is gender—only women die in childbirth or get cervical cancer, but many more men get lung cancer, and most casualties of combat are still males.

In the case of our mystery event, both men and women were involved (i.e., exposed to risk), and there were many more males than females in the at-risk population—1,690 adult males (76 percent of the total) vs. 425 adult females (20 percent). Looking at the mortality data in Figure 1.1 as rates, we can see immediately that gender made a big difference in one's chances of survival. Females were almost three times as likely to survive as males: 80 percent of the men died vs. 26 percent of the females.

What could account for that? A disease that affects both sexes but is much more lethal for men? For specific diseases, the death rates are called case fatality rates (CFRs), because the only people at risk for dying are those already diagnosed with the disease—that is, the cases. What diseases that affect both men and women would have such different CFRs for the two sexes? Maybe the sample involved in this particular event could have been exposed to the risk differently based on some differences associated with their gender— for example, a workplace where most of the men were involved in something dangerous, say, a toxic product that caused cancer. Or an accident where men and women were segregated in some way that caused the men to bear the brunt of whatever was responsible—an explosion in some part of the building they all worked in, but that housed more of the men. All but thirty of the 146 victims of the Triangle Shirtwaist fire of 1911 were young women workers, while the two factory owners—Max Blanck and Isaac Harris—fled to the roof and survived. Is that a model for our event?

Looking at mortality rates by age offers more clues. In diseases that generally affect both children and adults, usually it's the very young and the oldest who have the highest death rates, as is the case with influenza. But that virus acts very differently depending on the strain: the disastrous 1918 Spanish flu epidemic that killed over 50 million had the highest CFR among healthy, young adult men. In our event, all that we are given is the fact that there were 109 children under twelve and 2,115 adults—so only 5 percent of the exposed population were children. But somehow they had the best chance of survival: while only 31 percent of all the adults survived, 52 percent of the children lived (a 45 percent difference in CFR). What could account for this?

Most deadly events like hurricanes and infectious diseases also strike the very old and the very young hardest—people who are the frailest and least able to fight for their own survival. Again, it could be something about the children and the women that exposed them both differentially to whatever is killing all these people— maybe some of the children were with the women who survived, being helped by them. We still need more data—especially something that would tell us more about what common feature differentiates among these 2,224 individuals with such a dangerous exposure to a potentially highly lethal risk.

Figure 1.2. Survival Rates by Social Class for Men, Women, and Children

	Upper Class	Middle Class	Lower Class	Total
Men	33%	8%	16%	20%
Women	97%	86%	46%	74%
Children	100%	100%	34%	52%

Women and children survived at much higher rates than men in each social class, but within these groups upper- and middle-class women and children fared much better than the lower class, and upper- and lower-class men were more likely to survive than middle-class men.

Source: Population and Mortality Data from Official Commission Investigating the Event.

The population exposed in our event was a very mixed group. Their social and economic status is given to us as upper class, 325; middle class, 285; and lower class, 706. Another group, the largest, was not classified by social class at all, but we have information that suggests they were all from either the middle or lower class. Figure 1.2 shows that for these different social groups there seems to be a clear trend: being richer increased your chances of survival dramatically. Sixty-two percent of the upper class survived, versus

41 percent of the middle class, 25 percent of the lower class, and 23 percent of the others (suggesting their risk was similar to that of the lower class).

One of the most important predictors of any population's health is social class, which generally correlates to higher levels of income, education, and housing—all factors that confer protection against disease. We know that social class affects health and life expectancy—in the United States the poorest third of the population has a life expectancy about ten years lower than the richest third.

If we combine the risks faced by each individual, there is actually much more information to be gleaned from the data we have. Examining these factors together in a single table (as in Figure 1.2) allows us to combine several of our variables and show the risk associated with different combinations of factors. After all, that's who we really are—we each have a gender *and* an age *and* a social class. If each operates separately to affect life and death, we may now ask, how do they work in combination in this event?

From the tables shown thus far we can see that the factors that predict better chances of survival—gender, age, and social class— seem to act together in a most dramatic way. In every social class, women were far more likely to survive than men, but upper- and middle-class women were twice as likely to survive as poorer women. For children, the effect of social class on survival was even more pronounced—all of the upper- and middle-class children survived, as compared to only one-third of the poorer children. We can now see that social class was a lifesaver. Independent of age or gender, class affected every group's odds of survival. So maybe that is the key—or at least a link—to explaining these huge differences in chance of survival.

Hint: Location, Location, Location

While social class alone may not account for different survival rates, perhaps social class in this event serves as a proxy for something else that explains survival. Could social position reflect actual location? Sometimes the difference between life and death involves chance or circumstance—where you are seated in a car or a plane that crashes, for instance. Sometimes it's about decisions made by people on the spot—for example, when triage is employed on the battlefield. In the World Trade Center attack, where you were located in the buildings made a huge difference in odds for survival: for those on or above the floors that the planes struck—floors 94 to 98 in the North Tower and 78 to 84 in the South Tower—over 95 percent died.

While epidemic diseases and catastrophes may take many lives, they never act in a vacuum—the social characteristics of the population have a large role in determining risk or exposure to harm. In the World Trade Center the offices on the upper floors were more expensive to rent and had the most prosperous tenants. So what could be the circumstances of our mystery event that catalyzed the effects of social class so powerfully and still conferred substantial additional protection on women and children?

By now you may be able to guess what the unusual event was that took so many lives so unequally. On April 10, 1912, the *Titanic* left Southampton, England, on her maiden voyage to New York City. As befit the ship's name, *Titanic* was the largest ship afloat, the most luxurious ship of the day. The White Star Line called it "the safest ship ever built"—so safe that she carried only twenty lifeboats, with space for less than half of her complement of more than two thousand passengers and crew. The ship's construction in the Belfast yards was believed to have made her unsinkable, so her lifeboats were deemed a bit of noblesse oblige—necessary only to rescue the survivors of other, less invincible ships that could actually sink. Besides, lifeboats took up valuable deck and cabin space that could be sold to passengers.

By now everyone knows that four days into the voyage, at 11:40 P.M. on the night of April 14, the *Titanic* struck an iceberg, tearing a hundred-yard breach below the waterline. Soon the icy water of the North Atlantic began to pour into the ship. It became obvious that many would not be able to get into a lifeboat, and the life jackets issued on deck would not offer any protection at all when passengers were exposed to water four degrees below freezing. The "unsinkable" *Titanic* slid beneath the waters two hours and forty minutes after hitting the iceberg.[1]

Subsequent inquiries attributed the high loss of life to "an insufficient number of lifeboats and inadequate training in their use." As the epidemiological patterns of life and death reveal, we know now that there was much more to it. The circumstances leading up to the deadly outcome have been described over and over in print and most recently as a hugely successful film, with the event characterized variously as a tragedy, a catastrophe, and a preventable man-made disaster. Now a whole new generation knows the story of the *Titanic*, but as the romance of two star-crossed young lovers. Like Romeo and Juliet, these two play out the larger tale of social class and conflicts—with all the huge social disparities visible in the passengers and their place in the Victorian social hierarchy of the day—expressed now in where they were located in the ship when it hit ice.

On the *Titanic*'s maiden voyage, the passenger list included a mixture of the world's wealthiest, basking in the spacious and elegant first-class accommodations, while hundreds of poor immigrants bound for America were packed far below deck into steerage at fares a fraction of those in first class. The crew were placed in quarters even less commodious and even deeper in the bowels of the ship—farther from the escape routes in the event of disaster.

While there was adequate time for most to get to the lifeboats, there was room in them for only one-third of the ship's population, so two-thirds died. The shortage of lifeboats was indeed the primary reason why so many perished, but the lack of lifeboats is only the tip of another iceberg made of darker stuff: the brutally rigid social structure of the age—the huge and virtually inviolable disparities between rich and poor in Victorian Britain—and how that was reflected in the location and crowding of the various levels of accommodations on the *Titanic*. At the same time, the better survival rates for women and children, independent of social class, reflect the ethical customs of the time: women and children first. Like a social X-ray or MRI, epidemiology is able to look past the outer skin of a large-scale event to see its inner structure of cultural values, which are always important determinants of the outcomes of any epidemic or disaster—often more powerful in deciding who lives and who dies than the material circumstance surrounding the event.

The *Titanic* disaster is a perfect illustration of the power of epidemiology to reveal the inner workings behind events that take many lives. Organizing information this way exposes the personal, social, and environmental conditions that are the backdrop to all epidemics and to most large-scale disasters—especially of the man-made variety. These conditions often explain what happened to whom (and why) far more meaningfully than biological factors alone. Surely some characteristics of individual victims may seal their fates, but the specific context and history of large-scale disasters makes individual vulnerabilities and risks into epidemiology. Think of the faulty levees in Hurricane Katrina, or the system of sweatshop conditions responsible for the Triangle fire. The victims of these disastrous events were not randomly chosen for their fate.

The *Titanic* has therefore become a classic example of epidemiological detective work and is still widely used in teaching epidemiology to public health and medical students—exactly because it does not seem at all like an epidemic of any ordinary disease. But the epidemiology of the *Titanic* helps us both to understand the special viewpoint of the epidemiologist and see the power of the tools and explanatory capabilities of this relatively new discipline to illuminate important events.

Epidemiology allows us to understand large-scale disasters better, in ways aimed at preventing their recurrence. This kind of analysis can reveal the truth about the structures behind diseases and disasters—the arrogance of wealth and power in the twilight of the Gilded Age in the case of the *Titanic*, for instance. It can often act as the catalyst for progress and reform—the revision of existing lifeboat and shipbuilding regulations in the case of the *Titanic*, for example, or the fire safety laws that came out of the Triangle fire.

Epidemiology (from the Greek for *epi-*, "upon," and *demos*, "the people") is the principal tool of the science of public health. The discipline is usually closely allied to medicine and widely used to assess the patterns and risks for the most common health problems we face (diabetes, heart disease, cancer) and the effects of various medical treatments—especially new drugs. Its historical and most well-recognized role is to make sense of the data from new diseases, but this role has grown to the analysis of many other sorts of human catastrophes (wars, natural disasters, even tragic shipwrecks), as well as the health effects of human behaviors (smoking tobacco, drinking alcohol, texting while driving), and patterns and causes of mental illness, homicide, and suicide. By drilling down to get as many details as possible about individual cases and organizing these properly, we have the means for better understanding each of these very different epidemic problems now facing us.

The following chapters explore two other classic epidemics—cholera in nineteenth-century London and AIDS in twentieth-century New York—to help understand the specific ways that the concept and tools of epidemiology work. In the second half of this book, these concepts and tools are brought to bear on the topic of mass incarceration, seen as an epidemic—a plague of late twentieth- and early twenty-first-century America.

2

CHOLERA IN LONDON:
THE GHOST MAPS OF DR. SNOW

Cholera was one of the dreaded diseases of the eighteenth and nineteenth centuries, a deadly bacterial invasion that led to a very rapid and violent death by dehydration and kidney failure. Arriving in England on ships from the country's Indian empire, cholera accompanied the increasing urbanization and population concentration of the industrial age—the advent of the "satanic mills" of Britain's surging economy of the eighteenth and nineteenth centuries.[1] In 1848–49, a cholera epidemic swept through London, killing 6,565 people out of a population of 463,000. Then, five years later, in the summer of 1854, London was struck by another outbreak. By September, many thousands more had died this terrible death.[2]

At the time of these outbreaks, no one knew where cholera came from or how it was transmitted. There were many theories about what caused cholera and what made it spread. Most people (including many doctors) assumed it was the abundant dirt and foul air (variously called *effluvia, miasma,* and *malaria*) from the coal burning that characterized the rapidly industrializing city.[3]

While it now can be easily managed medically, by rehydration and antibiotics, at the time there was no treatment for cholera. No one had any power to help the victims, and over 50 percent of those infected died an agonizing death within days of the first symptoms. Doctors, priests, and families were reduced to ministering to the dying and attempting to alleviate their suffering. In addition, the medical profession of the day did not know how to protect themselves or others from catching it—one of the consequences of not having any testable hypotheses about how the disease was transmitted.

The question of transmission, the communicability of a disease from one victim to the next, is a defining characteristic of epidemics of infectious diseases.[4] Each case of the disease becomes the source of exposure for others and, possibly, infection of new individuals who come into contact with them (in contrast to noninfectious "epidemics" such as the *Titanic* sinking). The epidemiological question in 1854 was *how* the transmission of cholera occurred. And, since no one knew how to treat the individual cases, this question was the only one that really mattered. In the absence of effective treatment, prevention was crucial. Epidemiology, the new tool of medicine, offered the best hope for conquering cholera at the time, and for a hundred years afterward would offer prevention as the alternative to treatment for many diseases that had no known cure.

The nineteenth century was the first time public health and medicine were able to use the growing awareness of microbes—living organisms that were invisible agents of disease—to confront great plagues.[5] Scientists of the time had many of the right ideas about the possible routes of transmission of epidemic diseases (through air, water, food, or human contact), but many wrong ones too. Most crucially, they had little knowledge of how these agents actually worked to cause disease and death (their pathophysiology) and even less about what caused them to spread diseases across populations. They could now see some of the microbes through microscopes, but they desperately needed to understand these agents well enough to control their spread.

The still new epidemiological method was based on taking the time to carefully count and describe the individual cases of a disease and wrest the secrets of the larger epidemic from the aggregated case data. A simple system was developed that took the cases of disease and characterized them in a manner that came to be called descriptive epidemiology.

One of the founders of descriptive epidemiology was a pioneering British physician named John Snow. While Snow was as helpless as the rest of his colleagues to save the lives of those already infected, the London physician had worked out several ideas about how the disease was transmitted—ideas that were rooted in his medical knowledge and led directly to a plan of action to prevent the epidemic's spread. Snow saw that most of cholera's victims had severe diarrhea and suffered from dehydration. From his own clinical practice, much of it among the poor in London's Soho district, he knew these to be gastrointestinal symptoms—common problems associated with spoiled food and impure water in the age before refrigeration. These were general symptoms that most practicing doctors of the time could readily recognize.

Several years before this most recent outbreak of cholera, Snow had formulated his theory that cholera had something to do with what the victims ate or drank and with where those things came from. He was interested in finding the source of the disease and understood that something in the water or food supply might be related to the occurrence of the new cases. He suspected the water because of the geographic concentration of cases in certain neighborhoods—a pattern that always seemed to accompany the outbreaks—clusters of new cases that came at the same time. He reasoned that the thing responsible for the transmission of the agent of disease (whatever it was that caused individual cases of cholera) could also be the basis for the epidemic.

At that time, no one did surveys of people's diets or carefully noted people's habits to see what they ate or drank. And Snow certainly couldn't interview the cases, since most were dead on arrival. So he began to collect as much information as he could about the location and characteristics of the cases of cholera in London's neighborhoods to see if he could discern a pattern. In what proved to be a breakthrough approach, he sought out records of cholera cases clustered in different parts of London and matched these with information about each neighborhood's water supply.

The outbreak of 1854 struck an area where Snow practiced medicine—the Golden Square area of London's Soho, a poor and teeming neighborhood behind Piccadilly Circus. He sorted through churches' records of local deaths and realized that he could analyze a cluster of cases that occurred in any area. As he collected descriptive data about individuals, such as age and gender, he also included information about the victims' addresses in Soho, which would also tell him from where they got their water.

Snow already knew, from research he had done in the previous cholera outbreak of 1849, that all the different water companies supplying water to London drew it from the Thames River. He also knew which companies had their intake pipes located closer to the city, where a lot of raw sewage had already entered the river. These companies' pipes, as he had proven before, were the ones that carried water to the very neighborhoods associated with much higher rates of cholera. But his research had done little to change the economics of the water supply in the still rapidly growing city of London. The water business offered very little consumer choice: you got your water from local pumps where you lived, from whichever local company had laid its pipes and placed its pumps there first.

Noting the location of the addresses where people had died of cholera, he mapped all of the cases in one small London neighborhood of Golden Square, which had been hit with over five hundred deaths in just two months, August and September 1854. Snow became one of the fathers of modern epidemiology when he made a simple map of the cholera cases at each address—one small box for each death. He also mapped the location of each water pump in the neighborhood.

Even a casual look at the map in Figure 2.1 reveals a lot about the outbreak in Golden Square—the clustering of several cases in some streets and, of equal importance, the absence of cases in others. This simple observation dramatically changes the question from "What caused the concentration of cases in Golden Square?" to "What is the difference between the houses with cases and those

Figure 2.1. The Cholera Pump: Map of Cholera Deaths and the Water Pumps in Soho in the Outbreak of August–September 1854

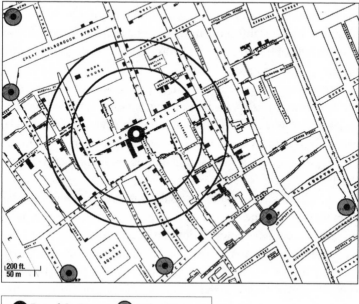

● Broad St. Pump   ◉ Other Pumps

This map shows all recorded deaths due to cholera in the Soho outbreak in late August and early September 1854, which took over five hundred lives. Dr. John Snow placed small markers at each address on a map—one mark for each death; the longer the marker, the higher the number of deaths at that address. All these deaths are in the Soho neighborhood, with the most concentrated in the Broad Street area (the large concentric circles); some addresses have many deaths, but others (e.g., a brewery) have none at all. It also maps the location of the seven pumps (shown as smaller circles) that supplied drinking water to the Soho neighborhood. One pump (the dark circle on Broad Street) lies at the epicenter of the outbreak and is the closest pump to over half of all the cases in this outbreak. It was subsequently found to be contaminated with raw sewage and was identified as the source of the outbreak.

Source: Snow, *On the Mode of Communication of Cholera*, map.

without, and between Golden Square and adjacent areas not struck by the outbreak?"

Snow made it a point to locate all the pumps that brought water to residents of the neighborhood. He knew the companies that owned each pump, and the sources of all the water pumps on his map. And there, right in the middle of the densest area of cholera cases in Soho, he saw that one pump stood out—the Broad Street pump.[6]

Snow knew that the Broad Street pump provided water from the Southwark and Lambeth Company, a company that took its water from lower in the Thames River than any other commercial water supplier in the area—amd whose pumps had more opportunity to pick up contaminants from all the sewers that emptied into the Thames River above it.

John Snow's simple map marks the birth of the modern science of epidemiology and provides an elegant example of the emerging power of epidemiological methods and reasoning. Once the question was framed as an issue of water, the map was exactly the right method for testing the hypothesis. With further investigation, Snow was able to say that most of the houses where the deaths had occurred got their water from this single pump—one of seven pumps in the area. Later he would learn that an adjacent cesspool was leaking raw sewage into this pump's base. He surmised this sewage contained human feces, which carried the bacteria that he suspected as the causal agent of the disease. The water from this well was teeming with the waste products of the poor souls with cholera living in the crowded houses that surrounded it, and, more generally, from the Thames itself. The disease was spread with every drink a healthy person took from the Broad Street pump.

Despite his previous published research on the effects of contaminated water, it took Snow some time to persuade people that the water supply was the cause of the cholera outbreak. The belief that the disease was a result of bad air (*mal-aria*) was still dominant at the time, and it was not easy to shift this belief. But eventually his efforts prevailed, and he persuaded the city authorities to remove the handle from the Broad Street pump so that the contaminated source of water was cut off.

Snow and his "Ghost Maps" helped to advance the nineteenth-century sanitarian movement, which was the watershed of the modern field of public health—the practice of preventive medicine based on scientific evidence.[7] After millennia of medical helplessness, and even though there was no effective treatment for cholera, epidemiology at least had some power to protect the public's health by preventing new cases of a still incurable disease.

Snow's work highlights many important principles of epidemiology and public health, especially the value of carefully counting cases and of sorting them out by the epidemiological variables of time, person, and place. While the location of the passengers in the doomed *Titanic* reflected social class and predicted each individual's odds of survival, in the case of cholera place also proved to be a crucial basis of increased risk for exposure to the pathogen (the cholera vibrio) that is the disease's biological casual agent.

But, lest we think that epidemics are one-dimensional, with single causes that can be determined and eradicated, it is important to remember that many different factors come into play and interact in any epidemic. Some of these can be tracked by understanding exceptions to the basic rule of the importance of location. For instance, in the same way that the Victorian belief in "women and children first" trumped the importance of place on the *Titanic*, at least one clear exception trumped location on Snow's maps as well. A closer look at the Snow map shows that one entire building at the intersection of Broad Street and New Street in Golden Square had no cases of disease at all—and it was only a block away from the infamous Broad Street pump. Why? The map's fine print tells us it was a brewery and workhouse. Many men lived there, but the brewery showed none of the deadly little squares that stood for cases of cholera on Snow's map, even though the water the men used was from the same system and was used to make the beer that they drank daily.

The reason the brewers were spared, it turns out, is that their water was boiled for the brewing process, and boiling killed the cholera vibrio. Understanding this exception serves as a kind of control, helping to confirm the notion that cholera was spread through the water system. But it also demonstrates an effective and simple intervention: when the water was treated (boiled), no cholera was transmitted. Today we chlorinate the water supply for this same basic reason—to kill dangerous microorganisms that transmit disease.

Ultimately, anomalies such as these highlight the utility of mapping, both proving the rule with the exception and reminding us that all epidemics are multidetermined. Even a clear culprit such as the Broad Street pump is part of a more complex social context involving location, the economic conventions of the era, and chance. And while we may not know what all the causes of an epidemic are or how to treat the cases, Snow's work demonstrates that mapping early cases—exceptions and all—gives us vital clues as to what causes disease and how an epidemic is spread.

3

AIDS: THE EPIDEMIOLOGY
OF A NEW DISEASE

In June of 1981 five young men lay dying in a Los Angeles hospital. They appeared to be sick with symptoms of immune diseases that were normally seen only in the elderly—and even then rarely. And they were all gay.[1] With typical medical understatement, the disease they were suffering from was eventually named acquired immune deficiency syndrome (AIDS), a concise label that objectively reflected all that was known or inferred about the disease at the time. The fact that it was acquired meant that it was caused by an infection with an outside agent transmitted from another person who also had the new disease. Thus the disease was infectious, not the result of some internal disease process like a stroke or cancer.

As we saw with cholera, every human infectious disease has an agent—a virus or bacterium that infects the human and causes the disease processes to begin. In communicable diseases, the agent is transmitted from one person to another by some means or mechanism—something that we call a vector. In a well-known example, mosquitoes are the vector for transmitting malaria. When AIDS first appeared, no one knew for sure either the nature of the disease agent or its vector(s) of transmission from person to person. But since those first cases were all gay men, sexual transmission was the prime vector suspect.[2]

While the agent and vector of this new disease were still unknown, the damage the disease caused the immune system was profound and could be easily confirmed clinically—observed as the failure of the immune system to defend the individual against the many biological pathogens with which it normally deals so well. These first cases in California were all in the very advanced stages of disease—most died within a few months of admission to the hospital. Doing their best to treat the flood of cases of this new disease was the first priority for the Los Angeles doctors.

The epidemiologists, by contrast, were focused on understanding the disease's vectors. Their goal was not treatment but prevention of the disease's spread. What were the specific mechanisms of the acquisition and transmission of the virus from person to person? That was the great challenge facing public health officials.[3] The story of John Snow and cholera illustrated most of these mechanisms—the acquisition of a disease based on a microbial agent that was transmitted through the water supply, with the pump being the immediate vector, the last link in the chain of infection that was moving through the population of London.

The story of AIDS follows this same paradigm, as all infectious diseases do. But what was the "AIDS pump"? What was the mechanism that spread the new virus? How did the personal characteristics or behavior of those who acquired this deadly new disease determine who was exposed to the agent and who became infected? And, most crucially, how could we use this information to stop the spread of the new epidemic?[4] In the case of cholera we could intervene by stopping the flow of contaminated water by removing the handle of the Broad Street pump. But if sex (gay or straight) was involved in the transmission of AIDS, preventing its transmission would be fraught with complexities and conflicts.[5] The sexual revolution of the 1960s was still under way in America. Despite the growing assertion of the right to be gay in America, homosexuality was still socially proscribed in this country (at the time of the Stonewall riots in 1969, homosexuality was a crime) and had become a major battleground of the culture wars of the 1980s—a potent political flash point.

From its outset, AIDS was identified as a "gay disease"— originally it was called gay-related immune disorder (GRID) or the "gay plague"—and so not only was subject to the rules of infectious diseases but also was part of a fulminating political struggle involving the contested sexual identity of a nation. What could epidemiology offer in the midst of that struggle?[6]

In the first years of AIDS, before we had a test that could detect if an individual was infected with HIV, we had no clear idea who was infected and who wasn't until they got very sick, when it was too late to do much about it. But because of the way that AIDS devastates the body's natural defenses, even these very first cases of AIDS were a cause for real alarm—no infectious disease before this had ever done such damage to our vital immune system.[7] While anyone can become infected with cholera by drinking infected water, it is relatively rare to contract cholera directly from casual contact with a sick individual. AIDS, by contrast, looked to be highly contagious. If AIDS proved to be easily transmitted from one person to another, the country had a problem of unprecedented magnitude before it.

At the time, when no one was sure about how that transmission might happen, fear (even panic) about the spread of AIDS was palpable.[8] I recall a tearful teenage girl in the Bronx asking me if she could get AIDS from kissing her boyfriend, since she wore braces on her teeth and sometimes there was blood. And a local public swimming pool wanted to exclude gays. Containment, quarantine, and even imprisonment were all discussed to protect the healthy from the sick; images of leper colonies came alive again. And the epidemic continued to grow.

We now know that this epidemic silently entered the U.S. population in the mid-1970s, spreading invisibly among gay men and drug injectors, who at first felt no symptoms to indicate that they carried the still unknown virus.[9] In most cases it takes eight to twelve years after infection with HIV for AIDS to appear as symptoms of disease.[10] It would be another three years after the first reports of AIDS among gay men in California before we identified HIV—the human immunodeficiency virus—as the agent that hijacks our immune system and eventually causes the disease called AIDS.[11] A year later, in 1985, we got a reliable lab test to reveal who was infected with HIV—very important because HIV infections initially give little clinical evidence of their existence.[12] While HIV is steadily destroying our defenses from the time of initial infection (which may produce a week or so of flulike symptoms), it takes many years to damage a healthy immune system. Only then does the disease become full-blown AIDS, at which point a compromised immune system makes patients increasingly vulnerable to a whole range of infections (and some cancers). After years of infection, most AIDS patients broke out in terrible skin lesions, lost weight, developed bizarre and normally very rare infections, and soon died.

Figure 3.1. AIDS Cases in the United States, 1977–2005

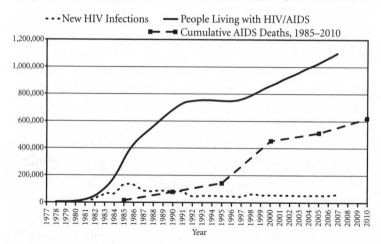

This figure shows the rapid growth of the U.S. epidemic in its first decade, followed by a stabilization between 1990 and 1997, as deaths equaled new infections. In 1996 effective antiretroviral medications became widely available and death rates declined sharply, even as the number of infected grew. There continued to be 50,000 to 60,000 new HIV infections per year, so the total number of people living with HIV/AIDS resumed its climb. Today there are an estimated 1–1.3 million people living with HIV/AIDS in the United States, and over 600,000 have died.

Source: CDC, "HIV Prevalence Estimate," in *HIV Surveillance Report: Diagnoses of HIV Infection and AIDS in the United States and Dependent Areas, 2008*, http://www.cdc .gov/hiv/topics/surveillance/basic.htm#hivest (2009–2010 data based on estimates).

se specific neighborhoods or their populations—that might ac-
nt for the concentration of cases in this early outbreak of a new
ase? If waterborne cholera from a particular contaminated
np on Broad Street was the source of that infection, what was
source of so many AIDS cases in the South Bronx?

All epidemiologists begin with the same set of questions—
t time, person, and place. I started with place: What was
ial about the areas of the Bronx where the AIDS cases are so
entrated? How did they differ from areas where the cases were
nt or fewer in number? Maybe it was an artifact; perhaps there
just more people living there. But there aren't: not only were
umbers of cases much lower in the North Bronx, so were the
per 100,000 population. Rates in the impoverished Mott Ha-
ection of the South Bronx were five to ten times as high as
verdale, a leafy and prosperous neighborhood in the north
e borough. How could we account for such big disparities in
incidence from neighborhood to neighborhood?

early, as in the case of the *Titanic*, we needed more detailed
mation about the localities where the AIDS cases clustered,
ore information about the individuals affected as compared
se who were not. The first set of AIDS case data we mapped
vailable only from old hospital records, most of which were
ted before AIDS was even recognized or classified as a new
e. These statistical records had none of the personal details
patients attached to the data sets that we had access to, so
n't know much about the individual cases except that they
ll adults over eighteen years of age, plus their gender and
de. In this way the data were very much like the *Titanic*'s
ger list, where we knew the type of ticket they had bought
t much else about them. But the *Titanic* ticket data became
seful, because they were a proxy for the passengers' social
he ticket type told us what part of the ship the passengers
eeping in when the ship struck the iceberg that night—
eir location determined their chances to make it up to

In the beginning, AIDS was a death sentence. We knew very little about the way the disease worked, except that once clinical symptoms appeared—weight loss, skin lesions, diarrhea—it killed almost everyone within two years. As always, the counting of cases was the first step in understanding this new epidemic. Figure 3.1 shows the growth of AIDS cases in the United States in the first thirty years of the epidemic.

This is a classic epidemic curve. It illustrates the first and most important defining characteristic of any epidemic phenomenon: documenting the fact that the number of new cases (the incidence) exceeds the rate that is normally seen. It both plots the epidemic's growth in previous times and hints at its future. In the case of AIDS, the United States went from zero to one million cases within thirty years of the first case reports. By the year 2006, AIDS had become one of the most important diseases in the world's history—a new pandemic (a disease that is spread over the entire world), with more than 60 million documented cases and 25 million deaths by 2010.[13]

AIDS Outbreak in the Bronx: A Case Study

These global views, however, are not the ones that tell us what is happening on the ground, in the communities where AIDS struck hardest. Like politics, most epidemic outbreaks are local—they start in a certain place and affect a certain group of people, beginning at a certain time. One of the earliest outbreaks of AIDS cases in America took place in the Bronx, New York. In 1985, the fourth year of the AIDS epidemic in New York City, I began to map the first AIDS cases in the Bronx. Plotting these early cases of AIDS in all three epidemiological dimensions—time, person, and place. This approach offered critical initial information about this new epidemic, even though all the big questions about what caused AIDS, how it was spread from person to person, and, crucially, what could be done to contain its spread, remained unanswered.

I did not go to churchyards or funeral parlors as Snow had done—they no longer kept such records. But hospitals did. And hospital discharge data were reported to the New York State Department of Health on an annual basis. Even before AIDS was formally identified, cases of immune disorders were recognized in hospitals and noted as such, along with other diagnoses, and with the key information on the patients—their age, gender, and place of residence (by postal zip code). These data and their geographic details were all available from Bronx hospital records going back to the 1970s.

Figure 3.2. Newly Reported AIDS Cases
in the Bronx, 1983–1984

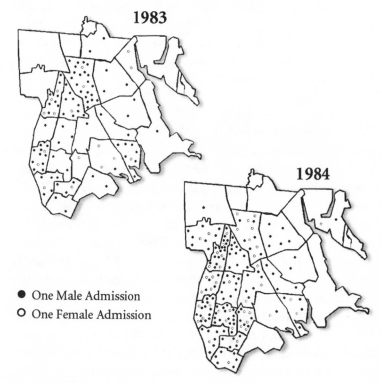

1983

1984

● One Male Admission
○ One Female Admission

Source: New York State Department of Health, SPARCS data system.

With the help of a medical student, Charl lected all the cases in the Bronx for the first ye demic, 1982–85. Using an old Apple compute the data and mapped them by hand. We mad of the first four years of AIDS in the Bronx: o (black for men, red for women), placed in the

Figure 3.3. Cases of Immune I
in Bronx Hospitals, 1982–

Year	
1982	
1983	
1984	
1985	

These figures show the rapid growth of cases of ir time not yet called AIDS in medical records—in cases may have been admitted to hospitals outs

Source: New York State Department of Health.

The data on annual cases form a tin growth of hospitalized AIDS cases (their i four years of the new epidemic in the Bron spread of AIDS in one early outbreak. Th doubled in each of the next four years, ri from 15 cases in 1982 to 323 cases in 19 eventually climb to 1,500 new cases by th 2005, 20,000 people in the Bronx were liv and another 10,000 had died, mostly in th demic, before we had any effective treatm

The most striking feature of the Br cluster of dots representing many cases borhoods, with a clear geographic cor Bronx. The subsequent growth of AIDS be geographically concentrated in the sa first cases—and as it still is today. What the deck and into a lifeboat, ultimately affecting their chances of survival.

Another important job was to frame the correct comparisons. What were the differences between the places where AIDS clustered and those areas of the Bronx where AIDS cases were less dense? The Bronx at the time was, and still is, the poorest borough of New York City. It is also (remarkably, considering New York's great wealth) one of the poorest counties in the United States, as measured by the portion of the population living below the federally defined poverty level. Poverty is what distinguishes the South Bronx.

To explore the new idea that the source of the AIDS cases had to do with poverty, we looked at other data and made more maps of the same Bronx neighborhoods, charting social variables rather than biological measures: income and poverty levels, high school dropout rates, and crime rates. Even a quick look at these maps reveals that the earliest AIDS cases show a clear correspondence with the greatest concentrations of poverty and the poorest educational levels in the borough. The Bronx maps charting poverty, poor education, crime, and deaths due to drug overdoses are almost identical to the AIDS maps.

But why and how does this correlate with the early outbreak of the AIDS epidemic in the Bronx? What is the AIDS "pump" responsible for transmission of the disease in these communities?

In the 1960s and '70s, the South Bronx was iconic for its poverty, deteriorated housing, violence, and drug addiction—when much of the borough went up in flames, completing the image of a war zone. "Ladies and gentlemen, the Bronx is burning," announced sportscaster Howard Cosell on national TV while covering the Bronx-based Yankees in the 1977 World Series. Beginning in 1969, I ran a drug treatment program that served many of these areas of the Bronx. In the years represented on our AIDS map, almost 50 percent of my patients became infected. Could drug use be a source of AIDS?

While we now know that heroin addiction and injections were a crucial driver of the AIDS epidemic in New York City, we were initially met with skepticism when we advanced this idea to our colleagues. As previously noted, when AIDS first appeared among gay men in California and New York, this new disease was actually called GRID—gay-related immune disorder. AIDS was the gay plague; all of the different ways it could be transmitted were not yet recognized nor understood. The idea that AIDS did not happen exclusively to gay people was met with disbelief.

In 1983 and 1984, my clinic in the Bronx brought doctors and scientists from the Centers for Disease Control in Atlanta up to New York to prove to them that this was the same epidemic as the one occurring among gay men: "Just look: this man or woman who shoots drugs is not having gay sex. See the tracks? See the re-used needles?" Yes, AIDS is a sexually transmitted disease. But it is also a bloodborne infection that can be spread by sharing needles. The South Bronx's shooting galleries, with all their communal use of dirty needles, offered a new way of transmitting AIDS: a mini blood transfusion.[14]

By 1983 many already suspected that AIDS was a blood-borne virus and that it could be spread by infected blood from transfusions and shared needles. And by 1985 we knew that over 50 percent of all hemophiliacs in the United States, many of them children and teens, had become infected from the blood products that they used to control their bleeding.[15] This meant that the blood supply from which these products were manufactured was contaminated. While the AIDS test was put to work right away to protect the blood supply (one of the first public health measures to address the AIDS epidemic), there was much infighting. In France and several other countries this *affaire du sang contaminé* resulted in prison terms for health officials who dragged their feet on blood protection.[16]

The Bronx drug treatment and methadone program that I started in 1970 and directed for twenty years had over nine hundred heroin-injecting patients. We looked at all the factors that could play a role in their risk for the disease, starting with the drugs themselves: the types of drugs used, the methods of use (especially injecting), the networks of using drugs and sharing needles and syringes, the use of shooting galleries, and the users' other illnesses.[17]

We learned about patients' sexual behaviors, so often affected by their addiction—many female addicts were driven to the sex trade as prostitutes—adding another risk factor to their injecting. And we examined the risks of transmitting HIV to others: sexual partners, children, and other household members who shared food, dishes and eating utensils, bathroom towels, toothbrushes, and shaving equipment. It wasn't until the fifth year of the epidemic that Drs. Jerry Friedland and Brian Salzmann did the first study showing that household members were not at risk from this everyday casual contact.[18]

But we certainly couldn't say that about all the staff who worked so intimately with the sickest of these patients—touching and holding them close, drawing their blood, cleaning up their bodily fluids, which we knew contained the live virus. We understood that the doctors themselves were at risk from needle sticks and blood from these patients, but for over five years we weren't sure about other kinds of exposure.[19] All of us worked in close quarters and talked to very sick patients in small, poorly ventilated rooms. Many of us cleaned up the patients' diarrhea and vomit when they were sickest, and most of us held and touched them when they were dying. By the late 1980s, dozens of patients had died and more were dying of advanced AIDS. We still didn't have any effective treatment for the virus itself and could only try to slow the lethal effects of the opportunistic infections our patients developed as their immune systems collapsed. Much like Dr. Snow and then-untreatable cholera, we desperately needed to prevent new cases.

Through the Eye of the Needle

Unsterile injections would prove to be one of the most important ways that the AIDS virus is spread. Addressing this problem would prove to be one of the most important ways to prevent it. The sharing of used (contaminated) syringes was as powerful a vector for transmitting the AIDS virus as was sex. Drug addiction became the most significant co-factor or risk for the spread of AIDS across a dozen cities in the United States. As a result, drug policy became AIDS policy, and the link back to drug use and addiction to heroin took on a whole new significance. Today, over 35 percent of all new cases of HIV in the world are related to unsterile injections—both medical and nonmedical.[20]

Even though the disease took eight to twelve years to incubate, by 1983 we were already seeing full-blown AIDS among many of our methadone patients in the Bronx. For the previous ten years of the still-invisible HIV epidemic, our patients had holed up in the hulks of burnt-out, abandoned buildings in the Bronx, Harlem, and Brooklyn, where many shared old needles that spread the infection of previous users very rapidly and efficiently. Now we were seeing the result. Soon all the neighborhoods where heroin injecting was concentrated became epicenters of the AIDS epidemic. In addition to all the well-recognized social and economic calamities associated with addiction and the drug trade facing the Bronx throughout the 1970s—urban decay, crime, and violence—the borough now harbored a modern plague.

And the same was true in scores of other U.S. cities, especially the old cities in the Northeast that had been home to large numbers of heroin addicts since the heroin epidemic of the 1960s. This included the rest of New York City, Baltimore, Philadelphia, Washington, D.C., and soon Chicago, Miami, and Los Angeles—although HIV infection rates among drug injectors decreased significantly as distance from the northeastern United States increased.

By the time the AIDS test was created in 1985, AIDS was already spreading rapidly through the population of drug injectors in the Bronx, where our maps now pointed to the true nature and location of the "AIDS pump" very clearly: the community networks of drug injectors who bought and sold drugs and shared contaminated needles. Most of the AIDS cases were concentrated in the poorest neighborhoods with high rates of drug injection, where most of the borough's addicts lived. And the majority of AIDS cases were among drug injectors, their sexual partners, and the babies born of women in both these groups. It was the sharing of unsterile syringes and frequent unsafe sexual contact (for money or drugs) that was the pump driving the local outbreak in the Bronx.

The addicts spread the infection to one another in the notorious "shooting galleries" of the South Bronx, where they "rented" the use of syringes for their shots. By the end of the day, hundreds had used the same contaminated syringes, acquiring HIV in the process. Once infected, they could easily pass it on to their sexual partners and, for infected women, to their newborn infants.

The AIDS test allowed us to see the rest of the HIV iceberg, whose tip was the people already sick and dying of AIDS but whose much-larger invisible base held ten times as many already infected. We administered the test to the patients in our methadone clinic, and now we could see the underlying infection, years before symptoms became apparent. It was a catastrophe: over four hundred of them (46 percent) were already infected with HIV. Still beleaguered with the many difficulties of treating addiction in the context of great poverty, urban deterioration, and chronically inadequate resources for health services, our drug program was about to become an AIDS program.

If the injecting of drugs such as heroin and cocaine was the AIDS pump in the Bronx, the analogy to the contaminated water supply of Snow's cholera was the blood of those addicts already infected with HIV. Each injection shared with an HIV-positive individual was a tiny dose of infected blood. The vector was the contaminated syringes they used to inject heroin. This drug paraphernalia was as illegal to have without prescriptions as the drugs themselves—a practical consequence of drug policy that made clean needles too dangerous to carry, and led to the lethal use of shooting galleries.

It took John Snow ten years from the time he released his initial reports associating the water supply with cholera to gain acceptance of his theories and get the handle taken off the Broad Street pump. But how could anyone take the handle off this AIDS pump? With the growing awareness of the links between AIDS and drug addiction, we soon had a perfect storm of personal fear (of AIDS and of drugs) among the general public, and growing antagonism toward the addicts themselves—driving them further underground. The impact of these attitudes would come to consume our efforts to interdict the AIDS epidemic by affecting drug users, causing more dangerous drug use, and thwarting our attempts to bring about changes in their behaviors. Public health professionals in the Bronx were met with sharp public resistance almost immediately—not resistance to dealing with AIDS per se, but resistance to doing so by treating drug users as though they had a health problem. In most people's minds, drugs in the Bronx were associated not with public health but with crime and the all-too-apparent local carnage of the war on drugs.

And, indeed, where there were drug addicts, there was also violence. The same New York City neighborhoods that saw over five hundred lethal drug overdoses in 1987 also saw two thousand homicides in the same year. This relationship between drug use and violence made it almost impossible to sway public opinion in a direction that would have allowed us to curtail the AIDS epidemic earlier in its course. The violence associated with the drug trade informed our drug policy: instead of treating drug addiction as a health issue, laws were written that essentially criminalized addiction. The default response to drug use quickly became (and still is) arrest and jail, not the effective treatment for heroin injectors that was already available, e.g., methadone, a drug that is taken orally once a day, eliminating the risks of injection.

The consequences of these drug policies had tremendous public health implications. When addicts became infected with AIDS, criminalizing them and locking them up perpetuated and expanded the nascent AIDS epidemic. New York's Rikers Island, for example, the largest city jail in the world, soon became the largest single concentration of AIDS-infected individuals in the United States. Drug criminalization and its enforcement undermined medical and public health efforts to treat these addicts effectively and failed to stem the tide of the AIDS epidemic.

Soon we would see that the driving force spreading this new epidemic among drug injectors was not the drugs per se. Rather, the political decision to criminalize drugs and related injecting paraphernalia created ideal conditions for AIDS to thrive. Every arrest of a drug addict further destabilized their already marginalized lives, driving them deeper into the most dangerous modes of behavior that transmits HIV. With its tens of thousands of drug arrests and the imprisonment of infected drug users each year, New York City filled its jails with sick addicts. And as the AIDS epidemic grew in the 1980s and early 1990s, another ancient disease reemerged in close association to all those prisoners with compromised immune systems. Tuberculosis had always been present, albeit at low levels in New York City in recent decades. But now it was facilitated by the spread of AIDS. TB was soon rife at Rikers Island, with (at the epidemic's peak) more than twenty thousand inmates crowded onto a small piece of land just off the Bronx shore. And soon they flooded New York's state prisons, where they remained for the next three decades (see Figure 3.4). Researcher Roderick Wallace called this a "synergy of plagues"—drugs, AIDS, prisons, TB—creating a new and very lethal ecology that has now become a global pattern.[21]

The decades since the 1980s have shown that death and disease

Figure 3.4. Neighborhood Concentration of
Prison Admissions in the Bronx: 2008

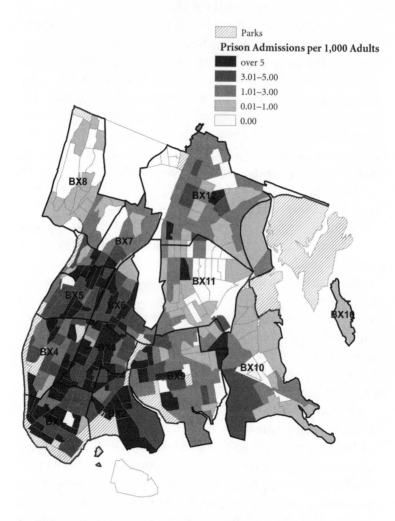

As AIDS cases grew in response to the rise in drug use in the South Bronx,
so did prison admissions from the same neighborhoods. Compare this
map to that of the early AIDS cases in the Bronx on p. 24).

Source: Charles Swartz and Eric Cadora, Justice Mapping Center.

are not inevitable by-products of drug use. We have developed alternative drug policies, called harm reduction, that are very effective in preventing the spread of diseases associated with drug use. Just as we instituted effective sex education and increased the availability of condoms in response to AIDS, we can make drug injection safer by providing clean syringes.[22] And we have learned that the ways we responded (and failed to respond) to our drug problems determined the course of the AIDS epidemic in America. So we can see that AIDS was a highly political epidemic from its first cases among gay men in California to its later home in the shooting galleries of the poorest urban ghettos of America's cities.

While the social drama surrounding the epidemic of AIDS was unfolding, AIDS medicine was making remarkable progress. By 1995 we had developed relatively effective treatments for the clinical disease of AIDS—antiretroviral drugs (ARVs). These drugs didn't cure AIDS by totally eliminating the virus, but they did hold the level of the virus in the blood of those infected to such a low level (especially if treatment was started early in the course of the infection) that the HIV could not do such devastating harm to the immune system. Today hundreds of thousands of individuals in America have lived with AIDS for twenty years or more. But even while the clinical syndrome AIDS has become a treatable chronic disease that is readily manageable in America and other developed countries with modern medical care, the AIDS epidemic continues.

In the United States alone, over a million people are now infected and living with AIDS or HIV—and more than 600,000 Americans have already died from AIDS. Ominously, many of the individuals and groups who are most vulnerable to AIDS are still ignorant of the nature of their risk. In consequence, the U.S. Centers for Disease Control currently estimates that fifty thousand to sixty thousand new cases of HIV infection still occur each year in this country—and have been occurring at this rate for at least ten years.

The conjunction of AIDS with sex and drugs created a political and epidemiological dilemma: America is a country where both drugs and sex (especially gay sex) are subjects of intense cultural and political conflict. But drugs have been so heavily criminalized that they have spawned yet another epidemic—mass incarceration. There are now over 2.3 million people behind bars in this country, and over one-third are incarcerated for drug use and related crimes.[23] And because of the association of AIDS with drugs and sex, at least one in six of all Americans living with HIV or AIDS now pass through the U.S. prison and jail systems each year.[24] It is the intricate epidemiology of mass imprisonment of the very populations already suffering from this contemporary synergy of plagues that we must now begin to unravel.

4

A DIFFERENT KIND OF EPIDEMIC

Beginning in the 1970s, another "unusual event" with significant impact on public health occurred. This one is very large—affecting tens of millions of Americans over the course of more than three decades.

Here are some of the things we know about this new epidemic:

- The population involved is diverse: men and women, adults and children, different social classes.
- The onset was very rapid—in thirty-five years the population directly affected by this epidemic increased tenfold, from 250,000 in 1970 to 2.5 million by 2009.[1]
- The effects of the epidemic extend beyond actual cases— over 30 million have been affected in the last thirty years.[2]
- Young minority men have been affected most severely: although they make up only 3 percent of the U.S. population, young black and Hispanic men constitute over 30 percent of the cases.[3]
- While this epidemic is nationwide, most cases have occurred in the poorest neighborhoods of America's urban areas—in some communities, over 90 percent of families have afflicted members.[4]
- Individuals who are afflicted are also socially marginalized and often become incapacitated for life—unable to find decent work, get proper housing, participate in the political system, or have a normal family life.[5]
- The children of families affected by this new epidemic have lower life expectancy and are six to seven times

more likely to acquire it themselves than the children of families not affected.[6]

Like the sinking of the *Titanic*, this new event is a disaster—but it is no accident. Indeed, it is the result of laws and deliberate public policies, fueled by the expenditure of trillions of dollars of public funds, and supported by powerful political and economic interests.[7] Although no known biological agent is involved, as with cholera and AIDS, this new epidemic exhibits all the characteristics of an infectious disease—spreading most rapidly by proximity and exposure to prior cases.

The new epidemic is mass incarceration—a plague of prisons.

Mass incarceration? The term seems out of place for America—a nation premised on individual rights and freedom. It conjures up images of brutal foreign tyrannies and totalitarian despots—widespread oppression and domination of individuals under regimes of state power built upon fear, terror, and the absence of effective legal protection. When we think of large-scale systems of imprisonment throughout history, we think of great crimes against humanity—Hitler's network of diabolical concentration camps, or the vast hopelessness of Stalin's archipelago of slave labor prison camps. Stalin's system established a model for mass incarceration whose effects penetrated every corner of Russian society, shaping the experience of millions beyond those in the camps—most immediately the prisoners' families. More broadly, it created an entire population living under the threat of arrest and arbitrary detention. This model seems foreign to life in our democratic society—a product of different times and faraway places.

Yet the facts about current-day American incarceration are stark. Today a total of 7.3 million individuals are under the control of the U.S. criminal justice system: 2.3 million prisoners behind bars, 800,000 parolees, and another 4.2 million people on probation.[8] If this population had their own city, it would be the second-largest in the country.

Figure 4.1. Incarcerated Americans:
The Growth of the U.S. Prison Population, 1920–2006

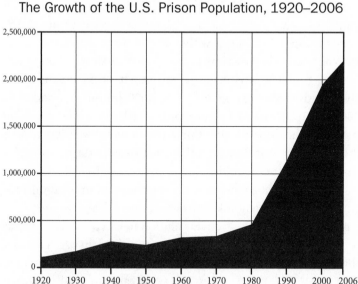

The U.S. prison population grew apace with the general population (averaging about 125 prisoners per 100,000 population) until 1975, when there were about 250,000 people in jails and prisons. Then it climbed sharply, reaching over 2 million prisoners by 2006—a historic peak rate of nearly 750 per 100,000.

Source: Justice Policy Institute; Heather Couture, Paige M. Harrison, and William J. Sabol, *Prisoners in 2006*, NCJ 219416 (Washington, DC: Bureau of Justice Statistics, 2007).

This huge system of imprisonment and the criminal justice system's control of millions of Americans is fueled by even more millions of arrests—an average of 10 million per year for each of the last twenty-five years, 14 million arrests in 2008 alone.[9] These arrests, together with the use of longer prison sentences, keep state and federal prisons filled with new inmates: over 600,000 enter prison each year, with an average sentence of four to six years.[10] This means that many also exit the system each year.

In 2009, 700,000 individuals were discharged from prisons,

most reentering the communities from which they came. But most are also destined to be reincarcerated. Circulating through the infamous revolving door of the system, 67 percent of discharged prisoner will be back inside within three years of their release. Even a decade after violent crime began to decline sharply nationwide (reaching historic lows in 2006), the growth of the prison system continued—each week in 2006 saw 1,000 prison beds added. In 2007 and 2008, a total of 100,000 prison beds were added across the nation.[11] Only in 2010, after thirty-five years of relentless growth, did we see the first decline in the U.S. prison population—a sign that this phase of the epidemic may have peaked.

Having described the unprecedented scale of imprisonment in America, we may still ask: is America's use of imprisonment really a justifiable (and effective) solution to an epidemic of crime? Indeed, with crime rates at historic lows, one might even conclude that all this imprisonment is a good thing. Or is it a problem in its own right? How can we assess the significance of mass incarceration in America?

Here is where the tools of epidemiology can help. By looking more closely at the data on imprisonment in the United States through the lens of public health, we can begin to parse the prison epidemic. Is crime really the source of epidemic-level imprisonment, or is something else driving this phenomenon? As is always the goal in public health, can we also understand enough about mass incarceration to learn how to contain and eradicate this modern plague?

Defining Mass Incarceration

Incarceration—punishment by imprisonment—is based on a set of laws established by any state or nation to assure public safety by the separation and isolation of criminals from society. By contrast, *mass* incarceration results from policies that support the large-scale use of imprisonment on a sustained basis for political or social purposes that have little to do with law enforcement. Hitler, Stalin, and Pol Pot all employed mass imprisonment—each presided over a process that arrested and incarcerated millions. Such systems are often part of massive programs of slave labor or forced resettlement, in which high death rates are a typical by-product. And some examples of mass incarceration are explicitly part of a program of ethnic cleansing or genocide—a tool of policy that intends the extermination of entire populations. But now, for the first time, we see mass incarceration in a democratic society.

The judicial mechanisms that states employ to accomplish programs of mass incarceration include laws and strategies of enforcement explicitly designed to imprison large populations. Methods include expansion of the list of criminal offenses punishable by prison terms, as well as harsher sentencing practices that impose long prison terms for crimes not previously prosecuted at all: being Jewish in Nazi Germany, or being an enemy of the state in Stalin's Russia.

This expansion of the use of incarceration (creating a vastly larger prison system) is almost always accompanied by worsened prison conditions, with more dangers to inmates' health and safety. In addition, the rapid growth of a larger prison system creates an expanded and more powerful system of "correctional" administration, which tends to have self-perpetuating features. These systems then add more and larger prisons, with better-endowed and more powerful correctional, police, and prosecutorial agencies at every level of government.

The Epidemic Characteristics of Mass Incarceration

What makes all epidemics important to public health is their large scale and the great loss of life or disabilities that are left in their wake. As we saw with the sinking of the *Titanic*, cholera in London, and AIDS in the Bronx, understanding epidemics includes understanding the many nonbiological, social factors that frequently determine who lives and who dies. These can be issues of social convention ("women and children first"), of moralistic and punitive attitudes (defining drug use as a moral issue and resisting framing addiction as a public health issue), or of turning a blind eye to social policies gone awry (as in the case of the consequences of the war on drugs). Failure to identify and address these underlying factors stands in the way of letting us cope effectively with any preventable disease and reduce the death and suffering it causes. Indeed, in the case of AIDS and drug addiction, we see matters worsen, with the epidemic expanding to new populations even as we develop effective medical treatments for individual cases.

Normally imprisonment is not seen as a disease, or even a serious problem for anyone but the inmate. Yet an epidemiological analysis of mass incarceration reveals that it meets all the important criteria for being an epidemic, a collective phenomenon that is more than the sum of its individual cases. These criteria include its rapid growth rate, large scale, and self-sustaining properties.

Rapid Growth Rate

Mass incarceration easily meets the first criteria for status as an epidemic—the rapid growth of new cases (increased incidence) over a short period of time. In the past thirty-five years, the United States has increased its incarcerated population tenfold. For almost a hundred years, from 1880 to 1975, the rate of imprisonment stayed flat, averaging 100–150 individuals imprisoned for every 100,000 members of the population. Beginning in the 1970s, laws and enforcement policies were put in place that caused the rate to multiply five times over the course of thirty years, to more than 750 individuals imprisoned for every 100,000 members of the population today. This growth rate is unprecedented in our nation's history.

Large Magnitude

The very large scale of incarceration in America defines its great public health significance, with tens of millions affected. The magnitude of our prison system has effectively made this country the world champion of incarceration. Today the United States has the highest rate of imprisonment of any nation in the world—possibly the highest rate in the history of any nation. By comparison, European countries average less than one-fifth of the American rate, and many average only one-tenth of it.[12]

The U.S. imprisonment rate, unprecedented in our national

Figure 4.2. International Prison Populations, 2008

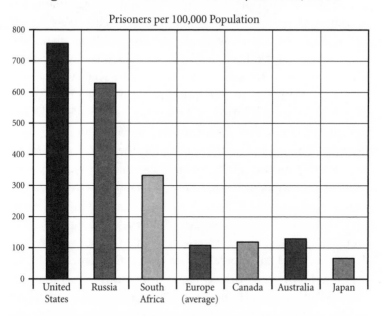

The U.S. rate of incarceration is the highest in the world—756 per 100,000—a rate more than seven times that of European Union countries and greater than that of Russia or South Africa.

Source: International Centre for Prison Studies, Kings College London.

history, is only part of the story. The number of those affected by long-term incarceration (in state and federal prisons) is dwarfed by the number of those arrested and held, even briefly, in local jails—another 14 million each year. In total since 1975, about 35 million Americans have been arrested and jailed or imprisoned, probably more than all Americans incarcerated for all offenses in the previous hundred years.[13]

In addition to the millions of Americans behind bars and the millions more under control of the criminal justice system through probation and parole (sometimes referred to as the "invisible" victims of imprisonment), our system of mass incarceration impacts an even larger population. These innocent victims must also be counted as an important part of the true magnitude of the epidemic. None of these additional millions has broken any laws, and they are not in prison. They are the "collateral damage" of mass incarceration: the children, wives, parents, siblings, and other family members of those incarcerated over the course of the last thirty-five years. In 1960, a school-age child in Harlem or in the South Bronx had a 2–4 percent chance of having a parent imprisoned before the child reached the age of eighteen. Today that chance is over 25 percent in many communities. Though innocent of any crime, the children of prisoners are also punished by the far-reaching effects of our system of mass incarceration, just as surely as if they themselves had been convicted.

With an average of about two children for about half of all inmates, over 25 million American children have by now been directly exposed to parental incarceration. Concentrated in the mostly urban neighborhoods targeted for mass arrests, they are the residents of the prison system's "feeder communities," where parents, siblings, uncles, aunts, cousins, close friends, and neighbors have all been incarcerated. In these communities, the epidemic of incarceration affects everyone—more damaging than the drugs that were the original rationale for so many of the arrests. In these communities, incarceration has become the norm, spawning successive generations of prison orphans and gang members. It is no secret these feeder communities are largely black and Hispanic. An estimated 50 percent of all the extended black and Hispanic families in the United States by now have had a member incarcerated in the last thirty-five years; for the poorest in both groups, that number approaches 100 percent. For example, in Washington, D.C., more than 95 percent of African American men have been in prison in their lifetimes.[14]

Persistence and Self-Sustaining Capabilities

Another hallmark of any epidemic is its persistence, due to factors that allow it to sustain its large scale and grow ever larger. Mass incarceration has shown this ability to reproduce itself (as infectious or communicable diseases do) by several mechanisms that keep people "infected" and create new cases in a way that has sustained its heightened prevalence over many years. Part of this is related to the vast apparatus created to administer the criminal justice system; part is related to the new laws that mandate longer sentences and keep the prisons full of older inmates for longer periods; part is due to the rules governing release and reentry—parole policies that lower the threshold for violations and ensure recidivism; and part is the result of lasting damage done to the families and the social fabric of the communities from which most prisoners are drawn.

Over the past thirty years, the nation's prison industry has grown exponentially to accommodate a growing prison population. Currently the prison industry supports one full-time employee for every one of the 2.3 million people behind bars.[15] The scale of this enormous "prison-industrial complex," encompassing over five thousand federal, state, and local prisons and jails, approaches that of Stalin's infamous network of prison work camps that incarcerated a total of 18 million people in the 1920s and '30s.

Not surprisingly, this huge American "industry" has huge political clout—with the expansion of prosecutorial and correctional workers' power, the growing number of lobbyists for these groups, and the many vendors who build and service prisons. Add in the financial dependence of many communities on prison industries in their localities, and prison budgets are hard to touch. Despite studies showing that there are, in fact, few long-term economic benefits of this "industry" for the localities that host them, prisons are often seen as an economic lifeline, especially in poor rural communities that have lost many industries to globalization over the last two decades. In New York State, for instance, fully half of the state's prison beds were once located in the upstate home districts of three powerful Republican state senators.[16] And in 2008 in California, the correction officers' union helped defeat a bill that would have moved $1 billion from the prison system to drug treatment, paying for rehabilitation and relapse prevention programs rather than prison time. The enormous and powerful prison-industrial complex that America has created is a growth industry, and it fights to sustain its "market share," always bringing new "services" under its auspices—most significantly, mandated drug treatment.

In recent years, budget crises in many states have led to the first decline in incarcerations in thirty years, via the early release of some nonviolent offenders and a politically mandated drop in arrests. In New York, this has resulted in a 20 percent decline in the prison population. But many of the sentencing policies that first built and filled these prisons continue unabated (fourteen states increased prison populations in 2010), with the focus of law enforcement increasingly shifting to lower-level offenses (e.g., marijuana arrests are up 5,000 percent in the last decade).[17]

U.S. prison budgets are also unprecedented in American history, representing the diversion of public treasure from other great needs—education, health care, social security for the aged. Averaging over $25,000 per inmate or about $60 billion annually, most of the money comes from state budgets. With several billion more to build all these prisons, we have created a large privatized "correctional industry," which, among other offensive aspects, offers new investment opportunities on Wall Street for operating "for-profit" prisons. With so many vested interests in maintaining the prison-industrial complex, it is no wonder the system has become self-perpetuating.

Another way in which the plague of prisons has become self-sustaining, according to new, cutting-edge research by criminologists including Todd Clear, is by destabilizing communities.[18] Clear has documented that crime rates in Florida communities with high incarceration rates can be traced directly to increases in imprisonment. In other words, what started out as a punishment for crime—prison—has now become a source of the very crime it seeks to control. Clear argues that massive levels of arrest and imprisonment concentrated in certain communities damage the social bonds that sustain life, especially for poor communities. By corroding or destroying this most common basis of social capital, mass incarceration sets up a perverse relationship: punishment leads to increased crime, as it replaces the moral mechanisms of family and community. These are the forces that normally function to assert social control, over young males especially, by the use of noncoercive means involving family and community.

Furthermore, because so much money is diverted to incarceration, other public services that might play a role in keeping down crime in these communities are defunded in favor of funding to build and maintain more prisons. Programs including health care, job training, retirement benefits, housing, and community development have all suffered a loss of public revenues, even as funding allocated for mass incarceration has grown exponentially. All these are worsened by the economic downturn that began in 2008 and which further restricts ex-prisoners' options.

Longer sentences also build incarceration rates and create a chronic condition of social incapacitation for those imprisoned, as they face severe restrictions on their rights and opportunities after release from prison. Individuals who enter prison and become a case in the criminal justice system today have a 50 percent or more chance of remaining under the system's control for life with recurrent arrests and periods of incarceration. In Louisiana, the state with the highest rate of imprisonment in the nation, about 100 of the 36,000 inmates of the state prison system will die each year within the terms of their current sentences—not because they have been given life sentences, but because the sentences they *have* been given exceed their life expectancies—the national figure is over 3,000 deaths per year. By contrast, between 1977 and 2006 executions accounted for 1,057 deaths.[19] Finally, in the United States, more imprisonment is accompanied by longer periods of community control (probation, parole) with lower thresholds for rearrest and reincarceration leading to increased recidivism.

Like the story of global warming and climate change, this epidemic of mass imprisonment includes many "inconvenient truths"—critical realities we do not care to know about—such as its sheer size, huge social disparities, and monumental costs. But unlike climate change, the scale and consequences of mass incarceration derive from relatively recent events and a deliberate set of public policies that continue to be defended as being in the public interest. Unlike many other afflictions, this epidemic is not caused by a deadly new virus or bacteria. It is self-inflicted and has required the expenditure of a great fortune, more than $1 trillion in public funds over its thirty-five-year course.

Paradoxically, despite its enormity and great significance for tens of millions of our citizens, America's mass incarceration remains largely invisible. Denial is the norm for the public at large, even in the face of the profound effects imprisonment has on the lives of so many American families. Compared to the burning issues of the present day—the economy, health care, overseas wars, and the threat of terrorism—imprisonment, even mass imprisonment, is only a marginal political issue at best. While the public is exposed to the spectacle of our vast criminal justice system daily via constant exploitation in the media—with scores of TV shows about crime and punishment aired each week—we by and large maintain the ability to look the other way, actively evading any moral responsibility for this system's existence. Perhaps that is because the story is almost always about "public safety," protecting us and our families, not the far more consequential and damaging epidemic of punishment we sponsor.

A public health approach to mass incarceration offers a new way to examine this phenomenon's significance and the role of the laws and public policies that, with or without intention, now sustain an epidemic of prisons and prisoners. Using public health tools and strategies, the remaining chapters of this book will take the full measure of the prison plague, gauging its impacts on our country's population and offering strategies for containing and eradicating this disease on our body politic. Data on mass incarceration will be organized to show the details of the epidemic's course along the axes of time, person, and place—tracking its early outbreak, the increases and patterns of prevalence across the years, assessing who is disproportionately affected and why, and analyzing the places and populations where the cases are concentrated.

With these data in hand, we will try to learn enough about mass incarceration's epidemiology to understand the agents responsible for causing it (the "prison pump") and the vectors that enable its transmission. We will also consider this epidemic's implications for the future of our larger society—implications that appear to run well beyond prison's effects on those behind bars. This epidemiological paradigm will allow us to see the rapid growth and huge prevalence of mass incarceration in a new way, as a public health and social catastrophe that requires urgent action. The final chapter of the book will profile some strategies for containing and eradicating America's plague of prisons.

5

ANATOMY OF AN OUTBREAK: NEW YORK'S ROCKEFELLER DRUG LAWS AND THE PRISON PUMP

Looking closely at a specific outbreak helps reveal an epidemic's underlying structure and dynamics. As in the Soho cholera outbreak, can the onset of one state's outbreak of mass incarceration be traced back to a particular source and point in time?

The start of mass incarceration can be clearly seen in the 120 years of data available on prison rates in New York State. Figure 5.1 shows the stable rate of incarceration in New York State over a ninety-year period (1880–1970) prior to the outbreak, where prison populations averaged fewer than 75 inmates per 100,000 population statewide. This time line clearly shows the surge in incarcerations beginning in the mid-1970s, a fivefold increase, which continued to rise until 1999.

What occurred in New York State to explain this surge of incarceration? All signs point to a new set of drug policies, drug laws, and drug enforcement strategies—the Rockefeller drug laws of 1973. New York's epidemic of incarceration, which continues to this day, began the year that New York's Rockefeller drug laws came into effect. Adopted in response to the rise in heroin use in New York in the 1960s, these laws mandated an elaborate new set of lengthy sentences for many drug offenses. In some cases sentences for possession and sales of small quantities of drugs were equal to those given for many violent crimes—rape, assault, robbery—and even longer than sentences for some forms of manslaughter or homicide. In an example of what would ultimately happen across the nation, New York's Rockefeller drug

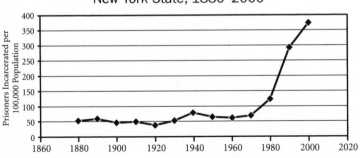

Figure 5.1. Rate of Incarceration in
New York State, 1880–2000

After nearly a hundred years of incarceration rates averaging less than 75 per 100,000 population, New York prison rates climbed to five times that rate in the course of twenty-five years.

Source: New York State Department of Corrections, Division of Criminal Justice Services. Graph by Jacob Hupart.

laws proved to be the "pump" responsible for the state's epidemic of mass incarceration.

New York's harsh new laws were among the first laws of their kind in the United States and became a model for the adoption of a range of state laws and national policies based on severe mandatory prison sentences for the possession and sale of drugs. Possession or sale of even very small amounts of drugs could bring very long prison sentences, whose lengths were determined not by a judge or jury weighing all the evidence and extenuating circumstances but by mandatory sentencing policies in which the number of years in prison was instead strictly calculated based on the weight and type of drugs involved and the criminal history of the defendant. Progressively longer sentences for second and third offenses were mandated, and in some states led up to the infamous "three strikes" provision—life sentences for low-level felonies if there was a previous history of arrest and conviction.[1] These sentencing strategies were initially promoted for "predatory" violent repeat offenders. As New York and other states applied this approach to drug addicts, their predictable repeat offenses ensured a vast increase in the pool of individuals available for prosecution and incarceration.

Figure 5.2. Drug Offenders Incarcerated in New York State Under Rockefeller Drug Laws, 1973–2000

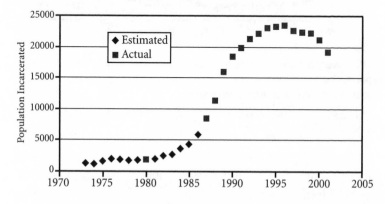

Source: New York State Department of Corrections, Division of Criminal Justice Services; Correctional Association of New York. Graph by Jacob Hupart.

Those targeted were by no means drug kingpins; the numbers prosecuted under the new laws (tens of thousands per year) far exceeded the size of any such group. Rather, it was the ordinary drug users—including marijuana smokers—of New York who were arrested and prosecuted. The police focus on this large group quickly created an explosive growth in drug arrests and prosecutions in the state and launched the state's epidemic of imprisonment, now nearing forty years of growth.

New York's dramatic increase in incarceration beginning in the the mid-1970s demonstrates all the key features of an outbreak of an infectious disease. It has a well-defined starting point, May

1973, when the new drug laws were put into place; an identified causal agent, the enforcement and longer sentences of the Rockefeller drug laws; a clear geographic focus in several New York City boroughs, and subsequent evidence of the diffusion of new cases outward beyond New York City to the state at large.

New York's increase in imprisonment is unprecedented in the state's history in several ways: the number of prisoners, the rates of incarceration, the geographic concentration of cases, and the extent of racial and ethnic disparities of the populations incarcerated. These elements constitute the heart of the epidemiology of mass incarceration.

Descriptive Epidemiology of the Rockefeller Drug Laws

As we saw with the *Titanic*, cholera, and AIDS, the next step in an epidemiological analysis of mass incarceration involves using the tools and concepts of descriptive epidemiology to make sense of the data both from the initial outbreak and from the ensuing decades of epidemic-level incarceration rates in New York State. Descriptive epidemiology allows us to visualize the data from this epidemic in a way that helps clarify its structure and modes of action by looking at details of time, person, and place. The descriptive epidemiology of mass incarceration should also help identify the epidemic's strengths and weaknesses, pointing the way to understanding its nature, hopefully well enough to change its course.

Time

We focus first on drug offenses, since we have an idea (based on the onset of the Rockefeller laws) that they are crucial. Plotting the number of drug offenders on a time axis gives us a visual image of the rise of drug incarceration—its prevalence. The curve that appears in Figure 5.2 for the twenty-five-year period beginning in 1975 is a classic picture of an epidemic's growth over time.

Following an initial slow, steady rise, after the implementation of the new laws in the early 1970s, New York saw a major jump in prison populations beginning in 1988, when newly legislated increases in penalties went into effect, lowering the threshold for longer prison sentences for crack cocaine (i.e., the adoption of tougher sentences for smaller amounts of drugs). During the height of the crack epidemic, from 1985 to 1990, prisoners incarcerated under the drug laws represented a third of the entire population in prison. By 2001 the population incarcerated for drug offenses in New York State under the Rockefeller drug laws represented an increase of 1,733 percent over drug incarcerations prior to 1973.

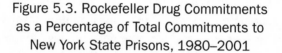

Figure 5.3. Rockefeller Drug Commitments as a Percentage of Total Commitments to New York State Prisons, 1980–2001

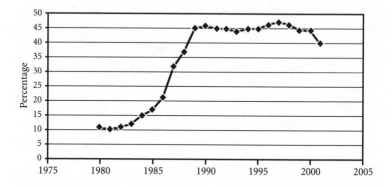

Figure 5.3 shows that, while in 1980 only 10 percent of all New York State new prison commitments were for drug-related cases, drug cases accounted for 45 percent of new prison commitments between 1987 and 1997.

Source: New York State Department of Corrections, Division of Criminal Justice Services; Correctional Association of New York. Graph by Jacob Hupart.

Drug arrests continued to sustain the prison population in New York State beyond the year 2000, although in the last decade New York has led the country in the overall decrease in its prison population (20 percent). Still, drug arrests are responsible for nearly half of all new commitments to New York state prisons. In addition, beginning in the 1990s—even after new arrests for drugs began to decline—the adoption of longer sentences for drug offenders based on predicate offenses served to lengthen the time individuals spent incarcerated, keeping the system filled.

Finally, increasingly strict enforcement of parole violations in the last fifteen years has meant a high rate of recidivism, which has served to extend the epidemic by re-arresting people for technical offenses, even though there is no new increase in crimes being committed. This has meant that individuals, their families, and their communities are affected well beyond the term of the offender's prison sentence per se. In these ways imprisonment is turned into a chronic condition, whose effects may last a lifetime.

Place

Within the state, the effects of the Rockefeller drug laws have been largely concentrated in New York City, although drug arrest and prison rates throughout the state have increased as well. After a century of incarceration rates that were comparable for the urban population and the rest of the state, in the three decades between 1970 and 2000 New York City's rate of incarceration grew to triple that of the rest of the state. Ironically, New York City supplies a steady stream of inmates for upstate prisons.

This concentration in New York City is as significant as Snow's discovery about the Broad Street pump.

In just fourteen neighborhoods of Manhattan, the Bronx, and Brooklyn, the past three decades have witnessed a state of war between the police, drug dealers, and drug users. And the police took many prisoners. Anthropologist Ric Curtis of the City University

Figure 5.4. Prison Feeder Communities: Neighborhood Concentrations of New York State Prisoners' Home Addresses, 2008

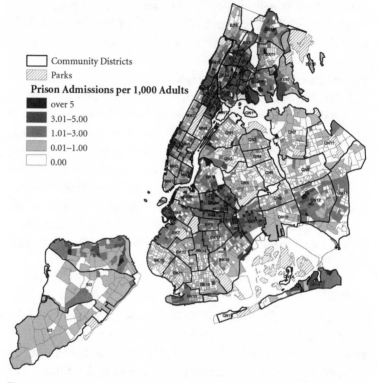

The darkened areas are community districts with the highest rates of in-carceration. Almost 50 percent of the people sent to prison from New York City come from about fourteen neighborhoods in the Bronx, Manhattan, and Brooklyn, where only about 17 percent of adults in the city reside.

Source: Justice Mapping Center, *Justice Atlas of Sentencing and Corrections*, justiceatlas.org; "New York State Prison Admissions, 2008," New York State Division of Criminal Justice Services (DCJS).

of New York's John Jay College of Criminal Justice studied the workings and outcomes of all the police sweeps of New York City's feeder neighborhoods—drug task force actions with military names such as Operation Pressure Point and Operation Cocaine Siesta. These sweeps resembled village counterinsurgency operations of the Vietnam and Iraq wars—massive shows of force exerted on a single section of the city, aimed at driving the dealers off the streets and collecting information that would allow the police to work their way up the chain of drug supply to higher levels of the drug organizations.

Of course, in a city as large as New York, many drug dealers simply moved to the next neighborhood over—which served to spread the street drug markets and their violence even more widely. As vividly dramatized in television shows such as *The Wire*, the drug economy becomes a world of its own, a world in which the good guys and bad guys are often hard to distinguish, and a world in which the drug users, their families, and their communities always lose.

Drug addiction today is more treatable than most cancers and far less costly than prison. But as the criminal justice approach to drugs eats up scarce resources, we see a marked deterioration of public funding for drug and mental health treatment services, and with it a decline in their quality. Those services that are left have increasingly become an arm of the criminal justice system, which has begun to embrace mandatory treatment as an alternative to incarceration. With 50 percent of public treatment capacity in New York State tied to mandatory treatment (with its risk of reincarceration for "treatment failure"), the fundamental clinical accountability of drug treatment professionals to individual patients has been subordinated to the goals of the criminal justice system.

Person

Finally, what can we learn from the distinctive patterns and characteristics of the people imprisoned: the profiles of age, gender, and race and the geographic concentration of so many cases in a few New York urban communities? The two tables in Figure 5.5 (one for males and one for females) display the rates of incarceration

for drug offenses per 100,000 for the year 2000, sorted for race/
ethnicity (often a surrogate for social class).

Figure 5.5. Rate of Incarceration of Drug Offenders
per 100,000 Population by Age and Race/Ethnicity in
New York State Under Rockefeller Drug Laws, 2000

Males				
Age Groups	White	Black	Hispanic	Other
Under 21	2	75	40	3
21–44	38	1657	1168	48
Above 44	10	329	466	9
Total: All Ages	18	718	597	22
Females				
Age Groups	White	Black	Hispanic	Other
Under 21	0.1	1	0.6	0
21–44	7	126	82	3
Above 44	0.7	22	25	0.3
Total: All Ages	3	54	39	1

The rate of drug incarceration for black males between the ages of 21 and
44 (the age group with the highest rate of incarceration for all offenses
in the United States) is over forty times the rate of incarceration for white
males of the same age. The rate of incarceration of young Hispanic men on
drug charges is around thirty times the rate of young white men.

Source: New York State Department of Corrections, Division of Criminal Justice Services; Correctional Association of New York.

Each of these tables reveals the disproportionate effects of
the drug laws and their enforcement in New York State by race
and ethnicity. Together young black and Hispanic men (about
30 percent of the state's population in that age group) account for
72.3 percent of all drug incarcerations.

These rates focus only on those arrested under the drug laws,
which is part of a larger pattern of ethnic and racial disparities evi-

dent in mass incarceration. Figures 5.6 and 5.7 compare racial and ethnic disparities in drug incarcerations to all other incarcerations in New York State prisons. The data show that the racial/ethnic disparities for drug incarcerations are 2.5 to 6 times greater than those seen in incarceration for all other offenses and that these disparities grew larger between 1990 and 2000.

Figure 5.6. Rate of Drug Incarcerations in New York State per 100,000 Population by Race, 1990 and 2000

Years	Rate of White Incarceration	Rate of Black Incarceration	Rate of Hispanic Incarceration	Ratio of Black v. White Incarceration	Ratio of Hispanic v. White Incarceration
1990	11	284	393	26 to 1	36 to 1
2000	10	359	313	36 to 1	31 to 1

Source: New York State Department of Corrections, Division of Criminal Justice Services; Correctional Association of New York.

Figure 5.7. Rate of Non-Drug Incarcerations in New York State per 100,000 Population by Race, 1990 and 2000

Years	Rate of White Incarceration	Rate of Black Incarceration	Rate of Hispanic Incarceration	Ratio of Black v. White Incarceration	Ratio of Hispanic v. White Incarceration
1990	58	637	384	11 to 1	7 to 1
2000	88	857	463	10 to 1	5 to 1

Source: New York State Department of Corrections, Division of Criminal Justice Services; Correctional Association of New York.

As these tables make clear, the rates for non-drug-related incarceration are also substantially higher for blacks and Hispanics in New York State. But when the inmates imprisoned under the Rockefeller drug laws are examined by themselves, the racial disparities are significantly more striking, increasing by a factor of five or more. Even in comparison to the disproportionate rates of incarceration for other offenses, the drug laws gave rise to vastly greater disparities for incarcerated minorities: by the year 2000, the 21,114 black and Hispanic inmates in New York prisons accounted for 94 percent of all drug offenders incarcerated in the state. In Figure 5.8, we can see these disparities in a larger historical context. For the century prior to the drug laws, the racial disparities of incarceration in New York State were quite real—with blacks being incarcerated at rates three to six times those of whites. But after the drug laws take effect, that disparity leaps to twelve- to fourteenfold.

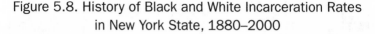

Figure 5.8. History of Black and White Incarceration Rates in New York State, 1880–2000

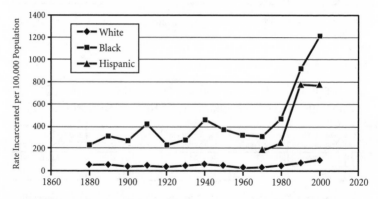

Source: New York State Department of Corrections, Division of Criminal Justice Services; Correctional Association of New York. Graph by Jacob Hupart.

The impact of these levels of imprisonment and their sharp disparities was dramatic and obvious very quickly. Their effects on the families and communities from which these inmates come are key to understanding the persistence and worsening of poverty and neglect of many social problems that have further contributed to the current epidemic of incarceration. As in the AIDS outbreak in the Bronx in the early 1980s, drug use is central to the prison epidemic. But this time it is not the biological effects of shared needles that have spread the disease. Rather, the extreme penalties and aggressive prosecution of drug use through the Rockefeller drug laws, together with selective enforcement focused on poor minority communities, has made it a virtual certainty that any New York resident with a drug problem—especially anyone who is not white—will wind up in jail or prison.

Incidence and Prevalence

Examining incarceration in terms of its incidence (the occurrence of new cases of a disease) and prevalence (the cumulative presence of disease) allows us to assess the epidemic's size, its trajectory over time, and the scale of its impact. In general, the relationship of incidence to prevalence varies depending upon whether people diagnosed with a disease continue to live over long periods or die quickly. The hemorrhagic fever of Ebola, for instance, is so rapidly lethal for almost all those infected that Ebola has a very low prevalence: almost everyone who gets infected dies very quickly. Before effective treatment for HIV and AIDS, in places such as Africa the total number of people living with AIDS did not increase much, even though the incidence of new HIV infections grew rapidly. Because no treatment was available, most people died soon after developing the disease. But in the United States and Europe today, over 75 percent of people with AIDS get effective treatment and can continue to live with HIV for decades. As a result, AIDS's prevalence has grown in these countries, with a steady increase in the number of people living with the disease. Also contributing to AIDS's growing prevalence in the United States is a continual high incidence rate: the fact that preventive efforts (versus treatment efforts) are grossly inadequate means that fifty thousand to sixty thousand new HIV infections occur in the U.S. each year (see Figure 3.1).[2]

Likewise, the prevalence of incarceration began to increase dramatically after 1973, largely due to increased incidence: more people were arrested as soon as the Rockefeller drug laws were put in place. Over the ensuing thirty years, prevalence has also been driven up by a number of other factors, including the adoption of longer sentences and harsher probation and parole terms. Each of these factors—arrests, sentencing, and terms of probation and parole—needs to be considered in assessing the exploding prevalence of New York's incarceration epidemic.

The New York State prison population more than doubled between 1973 and 1983 (with a 124 percent increase), and doubled again between 1983 and 1992. The epidemic then showed a peak in incidence, and its growth rate slowed to 10 percent between 1992 and 1998. Between 1998 and 2008 the prison population declined by almost 20 percent. Over the entire thirty-five-year life span of the Rockefeller drug laws, New York State's incarceration rate has quintupled, growing from 73 prisoners per 100,000 residents in 1973 to 386 prisoners per 100,000 residents in 2007.[3] (This is somewhat lower than the incarceration rate for the United States as a whole—445 prisoners per 100,000 residents in 2007—but higher than the Northeast average rate of 317.)[4]

Arrests

Arrests are the first-line cause of the increased incidence of incarceration. About 14 million arrests (1.6 million of those for drug offenses) are now made annually in the United States, resulting in about 600,000 new commitments to prison each year. In New York State over 437,000 arrests were made in 2010, with about two-thirds leading to conviction (over 90 percent of the convictions are the result of plea bargains). Of these convictions, about 50 percent result in a prison or jail sentence. For the rest, these arrests usually lead to at least brief incarceration while awaiting determination, if the defendant is unable to make bail. (Bail policies, meant to ensure appearance at subsequent court proceedings following arrest and arraignment, are another major factor in determining incarceration rates.)

The vast majority of arrests in New York City (as in most jurisdictions) are for minor offenses, so-called quality-of-life crimes increasingly prosecuted as part of community policing strategies. Even in the South Bronx, one of the poorest and most crime-ridden communities in New York, only 3 percent of convictions are for felonies.[5] The most common arrest offenses are loitering, vagrancy, and drug use or possession (crimes often set up by undercover narcotics officers posing as drug users interested in buying drugs). Together, these quality-of-life crimes account for approximately half of all arrests, with marijuana possession increasingly becoming the most common drug charge.

Although many of these arrests are for nonviolent, victimless crimes, most involve the suspect's being taken to the precinct, fingerprinted, and held in custody in communal holding cells for twenty-four to seventy-two hours prior to being brought before a judge for arraignment. Going to jail even briefly can be a searing experience, and these early encounters with the criminal justice system (even a night or two in jail) are not without significance. About half of the arrests and brief periods of detention involve job or housing loss, interruption of school or health care. For women it can mean losing custody of their children, and for immigrants (25 percent of Bronx arrests) it can mean deportation.[6]

Additionally, each such arrest generates a permanent computerized record. Even the most minimal contact with the criminal justice system creates a trail of data that eventually helps to drive the increase in prison rates. Once you're in the system, you stay in the system. So, while long-term imprisonment receives so much attention, the seeds for most imprisonments are the product of the development of a criminal record based on low-level offenses—often for drugs—and several years of pre-incarceration experiences. These early contacts with the criminal justice system, contacts that could be the occasion for positive early therapeutic or social intervention (as they are in many other countries), end up laying the foundation for future incarceration, in city jails and then in state prisons. Thus the arrest and detention process creates a growing pool of individuals who have become "infected" (often permanently) by contact with the criminal justice system.

Of the 437,000 arrests made in New York State in 2010, New York City accounted for 60 percent of statewide arrests. Of these, only 13 percent were at the felony level. The increase in arrest rates is primarily a by-product of New York City's focus on low-level quality-of-life crimes. Between 1993 and 1997, New York State misdemeanor arrests increased 30 percent (by 2010, they reached 318,000), while felony arrests increased by only 6 percent. Felony drug arrests in New York State actually declined thereafter, from about 56,000 in 1984 to 34,000 in 2003, and dropped to 26,000 by 2010.

While the total number of inmates in New York State prisons has declined by 20 percent since 1999 (to 54,000 in 2010), the decrease in long-term prisoners has been offset by increases in misdemeanor drug arrests and by the number going to jail each year. Decades of high admission rates taken together with the large number of people on probation or serving community-based sentences—parole or mandatory drug treatment—put the current total New York State population under the control of the criminal justice system at an all-time high of over 200,000.

Sentencing

If increased arrest rates for minor drug charges and administrative violations of probation and parole first filled the prisons of New York, longer sentences—a hallmark of the Rockefeller drug laws—have kept them filled, keeping the prevalence of incarceration high despite the sharp decline in crime that began in 1993. Under the Rockefeller drug laws, including "three strikes" and other mandatory sentencing provisions, between 1975 and 2005 the median prison sentence in New York State went from less than two years to more than five years. This meant that, in addition to more inmates entering the system each year, fewer were released. The system grew, new prisons were built, and old ones were expanded. As more inmates have stayed in prison longer, the prison population has both built up in numbers and changed in character, with the median age of inmates in New York State rising steadily. As the prevalence levels of imprisonment grow, mass incarceration comes to resemble chronic diseases such as heart disease or diabetes: once you become a case you stay one for a long time—perhaps forever.

Probation

While many arrests for low-level crimes do not result in jail or prison sentences, they do often involve a sentence of probation in which an offender is required to comply with a set of rules involving drug testing, curfew, restrictions on travel and association with other felons, and requirements for program and treatment participation. Because failure to comply with the terms of probation can lead to imprisonment, even arrests that do not initially result in a prison term often ultimately end up with an offender serving jail time or receiving a prison sentence as a consequence of violating probation. Thus prosecution of low-level crimes, despite historically low rates of crime, is the engine that drives the continued admissions and large overall population under the control of the criminal justice system.

Parole

Though the number of individuals released from prison in the last decade roughly equals the number of admissions, the prison population has continued to grow for a category of offense—parole violations—much less prevalent three decades ago. The sentences of inmates convicted of crimes do not end when they leave prison. Increasingly, the state imposes postrelease restrictions as a condition of parole, including regular reporting to a court officer, drug tests, and limitations on travel. These restrictions (and failures to comply with them fully) often lead to administrative violations and warrants that can cause rearrest and return to prison even when no new crime has been committed—at the discretion of individual parole agents. Computerized records allow police to access conditions of parole instantaneously, resulting in many arrests for parole violations in the wake of, for example, vehicle stops by traffic cops.

About 40 percent of all admissions to prison (10,000 of the 26,000 in New York State in 2006) are due to "administrative" violations, not new criminal charges. Individuals can be imprisoned for violating probation, parole, or conditional release, or for being absent without permission from a residence or other postrelease program or obligation. The most common parole violations are associated with failure of drug tests or violation of curfews. These policies play an important role in sustaining the state's high rates of recidivism—over 65 percent of prisoners in New York State are reincarcerated within three years of release, with 80 percent of these admissions for administrative offenses. In recent years, the percentage of new admissions to New York prisons attributable to parole violations has risen from 10 percent in the 1970s and '80s to 20 percent in 1997 and almost 40 percent in 2006. This is now one of the most important mechanisms of maintaining the size of the prison population, and evidence that the epidemic of mass incarceration has become self-perpetuating. It also points to an important way in which we could slow or even stop the epidemic—through parole policy reforms. It is especially crucial to change parole procedures to eliminate penalties for continued drug use past release (especially for marijuana) and to provide better access to effective treatment for hard drugs, including acceptance by the courts of opiate substitution treatment with meth-adone or buprenorphine.

But even with such reforms, the sheer magnitude of imprison-ment in America will continue to affect millions for years to come. In chapter 6, we will examine the meaning and significance of the vast scale of mass incarceration and compare it to other public health incidents and diseases.

6

ORDERS OF MAGNITUDE: THE RELATIVE IMPACT OF MASS INCARCERATION

Size matters. The magnitude of an epidemic (the prevalence of the disease or the scale of a disaster) is perhaps the most important marker of its significance and potential for harm. Prevalence represents the collective "burden of disease," a measure of the human costs it imposes on an entire population. If we argue that mass incarceration is an epidemic, we need to answer this most basic descriptive epidemiological question: how many people are affected by it—thousands, millions, tens of millions? Gauging the magnitude of mass incarceration allows us to put this new epidemic in a wider context and to see its impact and appreciate its significance both in absolute terms (the number affected) and in relative terms (how its scale compares to other better-known public health events and epidemics).

If, instead of prison inmates, the figures of the number in prison represented the progress of a new epidemic disease or the effects of a natural or man-made disaster, we would employ a set of standard methods to assess the numbers' impact and significance. Typical approaches involve counting the number of lives lost, the mortality rate, the case fatality rate, the number of serious injuries, the number of people displaced, the number of families and households affected, and the economic losses suffered.

But prison data are not normally viewed as collective public events that warrant such an assessment. Even as vast a program of incarceration as has occurred over the thirty-five-year history of the drug wars is not generally characterized as an "event" per se— nor is it generally compared to other public health events. Is it possible, nevertheless, to employ a quantitative public health method for determining the relative magnitude of drug incarcerations in a way that allows us to compare mass incarceration's scale to other events that have had a powerful impact on large populations?

Perhaps the most common measure of the magnitude and significance of any epidemic is the number of deaths it causes in a given population, known as its mortality rate. Death is the worst outcome of any epidemic, be it a natural disaster (a tsunami, an earthquake, an outbreak of disease), a large-scale man-made disaster or accident (a train or plane crash, a fire or building collapse, a lethal chemical spill), or a hostile act (a war, a terrorist attack). We use it as a benchmark to tell us something basic about the epidemic's severity. Mortality data have great power in public health because they are a universal measure of the human cost of any illness to a society. We use death rates to compare data from a single epidemic or outbreak to others and to give us a sense of any event's seriousness relative to other events.

But how are measures of mortality applicable to the epidemic of incarceration? With the exception of capital punishment, imprisonment in America normally doesn't lead to death—although in the subhuman conditions of prisons in places such as Russia AIDS and TB do take a huge number of lives. So how may we compare the effects of the large scale of mass incarceration to the epidemiology of other events that do result in death?

In order to create a uniform measure for the comparison of the impact of different large-scale epidemics or calamities, epidemiologists have created a measure called *potential years of life lost*. Commonly known as YLL, this unit of measurement represents the number of years that would have been lived by a victim had he or she not died in the epidemic or disaster. YLL is the number of years between the victim's age at death and the age that his or her usual life expectancy would predict. Thus, for the average American with a life expectancy of seventy-five years, a child's death at age ten implies a loss of sixty-five potential years of life; the death of an adult at age fifty implies 25 YLL, and so on.

This measure allows us to add up all the individual YLL figures for all the victims of any event that takes large numbers of lives. It expresses the net effects of the mortality impact of an epidemic or disaster, based on the number and distribution of the specific age groups in the affected population. The measure of the lost potential of remaining years of life for the 1,513 people who died in the *Titanic* sinking, for example, is about 47,000 YLL. This figure captures the potential life expectancy of all the children and adults who did not survive the sinking. Data on the survivors of the *Titanic* underscores the validity of the measure of YLL. Mary Davis Wilburn, the longest-lived of the *Titanic* survivors, died in 1987 at age 104. She and at least sixty-five other survivors lived to age ninety, underscoring the reality and meaningfulness of years of life lost for those who perished. YLLs can also help us understand the relative impact of mass incarceration. This measure allows us to compare mass incarceration to other disasters or public health events associated with many casualties and the actual loss of life. Such events may occur either in a single blow, as in the *Titanic*, or over decades, as with persistent epidemics of infectious diseases such as AIDS or cholera.

To test this approach, I calculated the YLL associated with the outbreak of mass incarceration occasioned by New York's Rockefeller drug laws. On January 1, 2002, New York State prisons held 19,164 Rockefeller drug law offenders—a number we can use as the average population for estimating the number of person-years of incarceration that occurred in that one year. Each individual prisoner had a different sentence—two, four, ten, twenty years—but each year in prison is counted for the population as one YLL. The median age of these prisoners was thirty-five, and their average life expectancy was sixty-eight years—significantly lower than the U.S. average of seventy-four to seventy-eight, because these prisoners were drawn from a poor minority population with lower life expectancy than the middle class. Extrapolating from these prison figures (see Figure 5.2), we can say that in the thirty-five years between 1973 and 2008, a total of over 368,000 years of imprisonment was meted out for drug offenders in New York State—that is, over 368,000 YLL. While spread over about 150,000 different individuals who were incarcerated (many for multiple sentences), this measure of the impact of our drug policy quantifies the years of life "lost" to incarceration under the Rockefeller drug laws in New York State. From the figures, we see YLL is a powerful measure of the laws' collective significance.

With the common currency of YLL, we can now compare mass incarceration to other large-scale events. If we divide the total YLL due to the Rockefeller drug laws by the number of individuals affected in a single year, the potential years of life lost to drug incarceration in New York State in one year (2002, for example) are 19,164. This figure is equal to the potential years of life that would have been lost if 479 New Yorkers (with similar life expectancies) had died in auto crashes. The total figure of 368,000 YLL for all thirty-five years of the Rockefeller drug laws in New York State is equivalent to the YLL associated with 10,606 deaths in a population with the same age profile and racial/ethnic composition. Using this measure, we may now make comparisons to two other events in recent New York history: the September 11 attack on the World Trade Center, and the AIDS epidemic—both of which had very significant death rates and years of life lost.

A total of 2,819 deaths were recorded by the New York City Department of Health in the World Trade Center attack as of August 20, 2002. While the ages of the victims ranged from two to eighty-six years, approximately 90 percent were between twenty and forty-five-years-old (with a median age of thirty-nine). About 40 percent of the victims were female; 17 percent were black or Hispanic. Of the victims identified to date, 64 percent were New York State residents and 43 percent were New York City residents. We can calculate the YLL for the deaths among those killed, using a composite estimate of a seventy-six-year life expectancy for a group that was generally more affluent than New York State prisoners and had a life expectancy over ten years longer. With thirty-nine years of potential life remaining, if they had lived out their estimated life expectancy, the victims of the World Trade Center attack yield an estimate of 104,303 YLL.

Figure 6.1 compares the YLLs for 9/11 with the YLLs for drug-related incarceration in New York State. It shows that the YLL of the Rockefeller drug laws exceeds by more than three times the YLL of the World Trade Center attack, in which over 2,800 people died: 368,000 years of life have been lost in the imprisonment of nonviolent drug offenders, as compared to the 104,303 years of life lost in the World Trade Center attack.

Figure 6.1. Years of Life Lost to Drug Incarceration in New York State, 1973–2008, Compared to Deaths in 9/11 World Trade Center Attack

Event	Number of Lives Lost*	Median Age	YLL
World Trade Center Attack	2,819	39	104,303
30 Years of Rockefeller Drug Laws	(10,606)	35	368,000

* In the case of imprisonment, these are potential years of life lost.

Source: The data used to calculate the figures above were provided by the New York State Department of Corrections, Division of Criminal Justice Services, and the Correctional Association of New York.

The AIDS epidemic in New York City offers another basis for appreciating the scale and the impact of mass incarceration for drugs. Despite a sharp recent decline in AIDS mortality in New York City from prior years (due to lower incidence of AIDS diagnoses and the effectiveness of new antiretroviral therapies that first became available in 1993), the AIDS epidemic in New York remains a leading cause of death for the state's adults. It ranks ahead of cancer, heart disease, and stroke in many age categories. This is especially true for New York City's young adult black male population, aged twenty to forty-five, where AIDS has been the leading cause of death since 1990.[1]

Because the AIDS epidemic in New York (like the Rockefeller drug law incarcerations) has been most heavily concentrated among minority males, we may fairly compare the race- and gender-specific AIDS mortality (in YLL) to those of a comparable Rockefeller population: New York City black males aged twenty to forty-five with a life expectancy of sixty-eight years.

In 2001, an estimated 242 deaths occurred due to HIV/AIDS among black males aged twenty to forty-five in New York City, with an estimated YLL of 7,986. In this same population group, the estimated YLL associated with drug incarcerations in the year 2001 is 8,085, a figure equal to the YLL associated with 245 deaths in a population of this age. Even in one of the highest-risk populations for AIDS in the country, in New York in the year 2001 more potential lives were lost to imprisonment for drugs than to the AIDS epidemic.

Figure 6.2. Years of Life Lost to Drug Incarceration Compared to AIDS Deaths Among Black Men Aged 20–45 in New York City, 2001

Event	Number of YLLs	Number of Lives Lost
AIDS among black men aged 20–45 in 2001	7,986	242
Drug incarceration among black men aged 20–45	8,085	245*

* In the case of imprisonment, these are potential years of life lost.

Source: New York State Department of Corrections, Division of Criminal Justice Services; Correctional Association of New York.

These data on YLL due to the Rockefeller drug laws suggest that thirty-five years of forced removal to prison of a total of more than 150,000 individuals from many communities of New York represents a collective loss quite similar in scale and proportion to the losses due to our largest epidemics or to an infamous act of violence and war. The national figures are even more staggering. In the United States as a whole in 2009, more than 400,000 individuals were incarcerated for nonviolent drug offenses—more than the total number in prison for all offenses in all the prisons of the twenty-seven nations in the European Union, whose population is over 400 million. This number represents the YLL that would be associated with 10,000 deaths of people in a similar age group. For the last thirty-five years the United States had over 7 million drug incarcerations with a minimum of 14 million YLLs. This is equivalent to the YLL associated with 350,000 deaths in a population of a similar age—more than the number of U.S. soldiers killed in World War II and all the wars since. To this must be added almost 2 million drug offenders on parole or probation today—lives not lost but often greatly diminished by the long-lasting effects of incarceration and its aftermath in their lives.

By examining the data of mass imprisonment as though it were an epidemic disease, we can see that it is in a league with the scale of the impact of other calamitous events—one of the criteria for treating mass incarceration as an epidemic. At least by this measure of the public heath impact of an event, our nation's drug laws count as a very significant catastrophe.

Epidemiology has been called a way of describing the suffering of human beings "with the tears removed." But the statistics and rates of imprisonment do not tell the whole story of 2.5 million individuals taken out of society and locked away behind bars. Equally important is the burden of disease, a measure of the human costs any epidemic imposes on the populations it affects. I call stories that reflect this burden "tales of prevalence."

I know of only one scientific study, done in the 1990s, that asked a random sample of 1,370 adult Americans, "How many people here know someone who has been in prison?"[2] Working at Columbia University's sociology department, the researchers were studying social structures and networks, measuring variations in the "propensities for individuals to form ties with people in certain 'hard-to-count' populations," including males in prison, the homeless, and American Indians. They found that overall, only about 1 percent of U.S. adults knew someone who had been to prison. (By contrast,

35 percent of men and 29 percent of women knew at least one airline pilot, of which there are 53,000 in the United States.)

Partly because of this study, I started to include this question in the many talks I have given over the years on mass incarceration: "How many people here know someone who has been in prison?" I usually specify that I mean someone in your social network or family—someone who has been in your house or whose home you have visited, with whom you've had a meal, played ball, and so on. In my experiences speaking with most professional and school audiences, about 5 percent would raise their hands in response to this question, and it was always under 10 percent, except with audiences who worked with drug users or in prison programs. Often, especially when the audience was doctors or academics, I was the only one to raise a hand; my brother-in-law had been a political prisoner in Chile, and I have a few American friends and colleagues who have been in prison for drugs and for political activism.

A recent Pew Foundation survey on imprisonment rates in America reported that 1 percent of all adult Americans were behind bars in 2008: 2.5 million people. The report made the front pages and network news, where it was presented as a "shocking" figure—an all-time high for the United States. But I suspect that 1 percent does not strike most people as a particularly large proportion of anything—it implies that 99 percent are not in prison.

As with the *Titanic*, however, the simple prevalence of incarceration is not the whole story. We already know that imprisonment rates are not evenly distributed across all populations. This important fact was to be powerfully brought home to me one day in 2004 when I gave a talk to a group of sixty high school students enrolled in a special program at the Albert Einstein College of Medicine in the Bronx, where I taught public health for over thirty-five years. The purpose of the high school program was to bring local students into the medical school to expose them to health professionals and their careers. The students would visit labs and see the clinics and hospitals, hear presentations from the professors, and get the perspective of staff members, with an eye toward interesting the students in careers in health.

These students came from all of the Bronx public and parochial high schools, but they were not typical. Each one had applied for the Einstein program and was selected because he or she was a successful student, near the top of his or her class, and planning to go to college. To be in the program, the students had to compete for a limited number of slots and get up to Einstein once every week for an entire term. And their parents were supposed to come in too, for a conference with the dean to discuss their children's academic choices and possible future careers in health and medicine. These were serious kids from striving, professionally oriented families who valued education enough to go to all this extra trouble to cultivate it.

The talk I gave them was held in a large laboratory classroom at the medical school. The kids crowded around large black slate lab worktables with sinks and faucets. There were about equal numbers of boys and girls sixteen to seventeen years old. I knew that the Bronx has the largest proportion of Hispanics of any borough of New York (and that was evident in this group), but I hadn't appreciated the extent of the changes in the Bronx populations that had occurred since I started working there in 1968. This group was black, white, brown, Asian, Latino, Russian, Caribbean, Middle Eastern—a true cross section of the city.

In my experiences teaching or speaking publicly about mass incarceration with various groups over the last decade, I've tried to get my audiences to appreciate the significance of the large scale of mass incarceration and how it might be visible in their own lives. So I usually ask my question early in the session: "How many people here know someone who has been in prison?" This time, to my amazement, every one of the sixty Bronx high school kids I was addressing (almost all honors students) raised their hands—100 percent of them. All had a family member, friend, or neighbor who had been in prison.

While a very simple epidemiological study, this experience impressed me with its great power and significance. The unanimous show of hands underscored the reach of mass incarceration in the place I'd been working for the last thirty-five years, but where even I had never realized the extent of its penetration into the fabric of the daily life of so many families. The abstraction of an "average American population" can easily obscure the meaning of any statistic. In places such as the Bronx, the high prevalence of incarceration is a day-to-day reality, not a statistic, and it is a reality that truly feels epidemic. It is all too simple for those of us largely untouched by mass incarceration to underestimate the true scale and reach of imprisonment in America. This makes it very easy to avoid coming to terms with it as the vast but (for most Americans) largely invisible problem it is. What was brought home to me that day by the high school kids was the disproportionate significance of mass incarceration where it is concentrated: in places such as the Bronx. In these communities, every family—even those of this select group of students—knows someone who is or has been in prison.

7

A SELF-SUSTAINING EPIDEMIC: MODES OF REPRODUCTION

We already know that an epidemic is different in important ways from the sum of its individual cases. An epidemic disease produces large-scale effects that go beyond its clinical expression in single cases and can lead to significant social consequences. We have seen how the explosive growth and large scale of mass incarceration in America over the last thirty-five years are among the things that define it as an epidemic. Another crucial and defining characteristic of an epidemic is its ability to sustain itself by creating new cases—becoming contagious (communicable from person to person) and spreading to new populations and locations. As in other epidemics, the collective effects of mass incarceration transcend those of individual punishment, lending it different and more harmful (even lethal) consequences—including increased risk of contagion.

For any communicable disease to sustain itself and grow, it must create new cases at a rate that exceeds the number of cases that are either cured or die from the disease. An epidemic's "rate of reproduction" is commonly represented as R. If an epidemic is growing, we say that R equals more than 1 ($R > 1$); if R is less than 1 ($R < 1$), the epidemic is shrinking. The epidemiologist's job is to identify the factors and conditions that determine the reproductive rate of any epidemic, first by isolating the specific mechanisms responsible for creating new cases (the biological causes of the illness and the means of transmission) and then by figuring out how to intervene to bring R below 1.

In the system of descriptive epidemiology we used to look at the *Titanic* data and AIDS, we considered three variables: time, person, and place. These three dimensions give us a systematic way to count, characterize, and map the individual cases that have occurred. They allow us to understand the patterns of prevalence and incidence of an epidemic. But in public health we want to go beyond description; we want to understand *causes*, including the biology of the agent's action, how the agent is transmitted, and vital social and environmental mechanisms that can help us to contain or stop epidemic growth. These are the pieces of information we need to influence the epidemic's reproduction. This methodology is called *analytic epidemiology*, where we use another trio of factors—the "epidemiological triad"—for considering new epidemics and their mechanisms of reproduction.

The epidemiological triad is composed of the three essential components of any epidemic: agent, host, and environment. The agent is the specific biological cause of the disease—HIV, the cholera vibrio, the carcinogens in tobacco smoke. The host (e.g., a human) is infected by exposure to the agent. Epidemiologists are especially interested in the different characteristics of hosts (individuals and populations) that put them most at risk for being exposed to the agent and acquiring it. For example, the elderly have an escalated risk of catching the flu because of their weakened immune systems and lungs. Finally, the environment (e.g., air, water, food, or blood) is what carries the agent or makes its transmission possible. Epidemiologists are most interested in the aspects of the environment that either allow the disease to spread from person to person, causing the epidemic to grow, or limit it by being inhospitable to the agent's survival or spread.

Mass incarceration reproduces itself in at least three distinct ways, all resulting in more individuals spending more time in the criminal justice system. First, the criminalization of drugs and the use of large-scale arrests for low-level drug offenders mean that millions of individuals a year—most of them young men of color—are "infected" by exposure to the criminal justice system, most often by arrest at a young age.[1] Many of those infected by these early encounters with the criminal justice system go on to serve more time in prison for other, more serious crimes later in life.

Second, massive imprisonment of young men and women, most of whom are parents, has now created several generations of "children of the incarcerated."[2] These young people, who grow up without access to at least one parent for a significant portion of their childhood, are affected both psychologically and socially, including being placed at extremely high risk themselves of becoming prisoners later in life.

And third, mass incarceration, concentrated as it is in specific urban communities, alters the ecology of those neighborhoods irreparably, fostering contagion by undermining the social and family support structures that are especially important for the poorest populations. Residents of neighborhoods targeted in the war on drugs are arrested at levels that destabilize and damage the social fabric that typically keeps individuals functioning as law-abiding citizens in their own communities. This effect in turn perpetuates drug markets, crime, and mass incarceration.[3]

Applying the tools of analytic epidemiology to mass incarceration can help us understand each element of this epidemic. Arrests and incarceration under drug laws are the most important agent of transmission that creates new cases of incarceration; the highest-risk host populations are minority drug users (who are the most vulnerable to high rates of drug arrest and imprisonment); and the enabling environment is the political and policy regimes responsible for the set of laws that criminalize drug use—the rules and sentencing practices of the war on drugs. Framing it in this way, it is clear that the criminalization of drug use and the deployment of the full force of the greatly enlarged criminal justice system to enforce our drug policies is the "pump" that has caused and sustains the epidemic of mass incarceration. This is most apparent in poor urban corners of America, driving the reproductive rate (R) of this new epidemic above 1, to the point where mass incarceration now bears all the features of a self-perpetuating epidemic.

The next step is to identify mass incarceration's mechanisms of reproduction—the specific features that account for a reproduction rate greater than 1. To accomplish this we must first measure the extent of any individual's and population's exposure to the criminal justice system. We will therefore consider various ways in which unusually high levels of exposure to arrest and imprisonment may serve to create new cases at a rate that makes the epidemic of incarceration self-sustaining.

The concept of exposure is used in public health to identify and measure the risk of an agent infecting a host; more exposure implies more risk of infection. When it is applied to bacteria, viruses, or environmental hazards (such as asbestos, cigarette smoke, or mercury), we readily appreciate the sequence of cause and effect—a person is exposed to HIV by sex or contaminated needles; inhaling tobacco smoke causes cancer. The dangerous effects of any exposure and its potential to do harm (to individuals and populations) are a function of the level of the exposure. How likely are you to contract the flu through one exposure to the virus on a crowded bus, or to become infected with HIV from a single sexual encounter? For exposures to toxins or other dangerous substances—drugs, cigarette smoke, chemical fumes—we are concerned with the level of exposure, or dosage. For most toxins, we are accustomed to using the amount of exposure as a measure of risk or hazard—dose relationships are used for gauging the effects of illicit drugs and prescribed medications, as well as dangerous exposures such as radiation and tobacco smoke.

The medieval physician (and alchemist) Paracelsus put it simply: "The dose makes the poison." He understood that the difference between a medication and a poison could be simply a matter of the amount to which a person is exposed. Things that are helpful or tolerable in small doses can kill in large enough doses. This is true of most drugs, some foods, and even water.

Levels of dosage or exposure are also useful ways to think about incarceration. We speak of a "dose of punishment" as though it were medicine. But is it a helpful or harmful dose? This idea of exposure allows us to consider the effects of incarceration measured as a function of its duration, frequency, and severity as experienced by any individual. We may measure the doses of punishment across the life span of individuals, for example as the number of arrests or periods of time spent in prison.

But we may also measure the extent of exposure to this agent for an entire population. As with the level of any other risky exposure for a population, involvement in the criminal justice system (arrest, imprisonment, parole) is an exposure of humans to a potentially harmful agent. When the dose becomes too strong for

Figure 7.1. The Tsunami: Percentage of Adults Ever Incarcerated in State or Federal Prison, by Year of Birth and Age

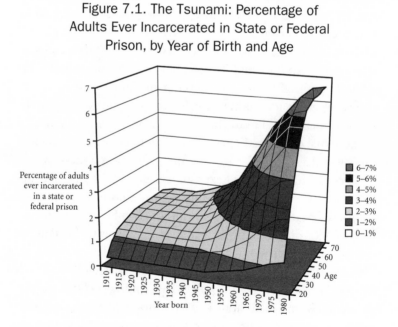

Source: Thomas P. Bonczar and Allen J. Beck, "Lifetime Likelihood of Going to State or Federal Prison," Bureau of Justice Statistics, March 1997, NCJ 160092, http://bjs.ojp .usdoj.gov/content/pub/pdf/Llgsfp.pdf.

an individual or any population, as it has become with incarceration in many communities, the effect is similar to a toxic exposure. Figure 7.1 shows this exposure generally for the entire U.S. population born after 1910—successive birth cohorts exposed to increasingly high rates of incarceration—the epidemic as a thirty-year tsunami of punishment washing across the American people.

We all have been exposed to a dose of punishment—meted out by parents, teachers, bosses—most times without being "poisoned." But is there a point where the level or dose of punishment is too severe for an individual, for a community, or for an entire society? Is there a "just right" amount of punishment? Clearly, high doses of punishment (especially cruel punishment such as torture or harsh conditions of imprisonment) can be both physically and mentally damaging for individuals. Some forms of punishment can cause physical and psychological damage that perseveres afterward and can scar for life. The possibility of long-lasting harm is inherent in the idea of posttraumatic response—a notion we now routinely invoke for understanding the damages experienced by many war veterans or by chronically abused children. Does punishment, when it is administered to an entire population (for example, via a massive level of incarceration in a community) equal a collectively damaging or toxic exposure, leaving a trail of posttraumatic effects?

The following case studies describe large campaigns involving massive arrest and incarceration under drug war policies and policing practices in two small Texas communities.

San Augustine and Tulia, Texas

The state of Texas is a highly punitive environment that now operates a criminal justice system of 156,000 prison beds for 24 million citizens[4]—one of the highest rates of imprisonment in the United States. Journalist Scott Henson reports that Texas "has criminalized so many different activities that [it] now has 2,324 separate felonies on the books, including 11 involving oysters."[5] While other states were looking for ways to reduce prison populations, Texas built more prisons. In 2007, Lieutenant Governor David Dewhurst claimed that Texas needed more prisons because of "population growth." But from 1978 until 2004, the Texas prison population increased 573 percent (from 22,439 to 151,059), while the state's total population increased just 67 percent (from 13.5 million to 22.5 million)—a prison growth rate more than seven times that of its population growth.[6]

Two Texas drug enforcement cases give a sense of how these statistics translate on the ground, and how aggressive (and often corrupt) drug war policies look in action. In the summer of 1994, an article by reporter William Finnegan appeared in the *New Yorker* magazine describing a "battle" fought at the height of the drug wars in Texas, in which the goal of state and local law enforcement was to prosecute and incarcerate as many drug users as possible.[7] An allegedly widespread cocaine trafficking operation in the east Texas town and county of San Augustine was "taken down" in a big drug bust called Operation White Tornado. A press conference was held to showcase the work of the two hundred agents from local, state, and federal law enforcement agencies who had arrested twenty-five local residents—mostly poor blacks. At that conference, former sheriff Nathan Tidal and the U.S. attorney for the Eastern District of Texas announced that the local drug trade had been "what you would expect to find in a major metropolitan area." They said that seventy-five pounds of cocaine—with a street value of more than $3 million—had been moving through San Augustine each week.

Yet months of surveillance, undercover work, and the raid itself netted only five ounces of cocaine. All the claims turned out to be based on false testimony and evidence planted by informants and police agents. Ultimately, this case was a prototype for many of the large-scale drug busts of small-time drug dealers that would occur over the next decade, filling our prisons with users portrayed (and prosecuted) as dealers.

I thought of this story five years later, when I first heard about a drug bust in Tulia, Texas—another hardscrabble town—that seemed to have much in common with the San Augustine case. In 1999, forty-six Tulia residents were arrested on felony drug charges after what *New York Times* columnist Bob Herbert called "an absurd 'deep undercover' investigation by a clownish officer named Tom Coleman." [8]

The men and women of Tulia targeted by Coleman (about 50 percent of the town's poor blacks) were characterized as "major drug traffickers." But no drugs, guns, or money were ever recovered when these residents were rounded up, publicly humiliated, and paraded before the news media, which had been alerted in advance to the big bust. Herbert described the subsequent trials as "pro forma proceedings in which convictions were a foregone conclusion . . . [that] resulted in grotesque sentences"—in some of the early cases, sentences of ninety years or more. These first sentences were then used to intimidate the remaining thirty-eight defendants and pressure them to plead guilty in return for lesser punishment—still sentences of five or more years in most cases. Once again, none of the allegations used to justify the vast campaign proved to be true. But the tales of entrapment, perjury, arrest, conviction, and abuse of sentencing principles were all too real. Forty-six individuals collectively spent a total of over 120 years in Texas prisons while the battle to exonerate them was fought in the courts and in the press. They ultimately had their sentences overturned. Herbert tells us of one of those jailed, Joe Moore, "a pig farmer, now in his 60's, who was sentenced to 90 years. I remember standing outside his vacant and absolute ruin of a house, his shack, and thinking, 'This has to be the most poverty-stricken drug kingpin ever.'" The impoverished "Mr. Moore nearly died from illness while in prison." [9]

Coleman's activities in Tulia have since been completely discredited. He was indicted for perjury, a charge to which he eventually confessed in a plea bargain agreement that let him off without any jail time. Prosecutors subsequently said that they had made "a terrible mistake in relying on Mr. Coleman's uncorroborated testimony" and eventually agreed that all convictions, including those of individuals who had pleaded guilty, should be overturned. Every branch of the Texas state government has now acknowledged, in one form or another, that the Tulia defendants were railroaded.[10] The events in Tulia demonstrate the dangers of law enforcement campaigns driven by mass drug arrests. They show how such campaigns reach far beyond individual punishments for individual crimes, at times fabricating cases to support the structure and tactics of the war on drugs. These examples from Texas illustrate the extent to which even low-level drug offenses involving minuscule amounts of drugs and communities of the very poorest drug users become the low-hanging fruit for the most aggressive and punitive drug enforcement strategies and tactics.

Criminalization of Low-Level Drug Offenses

The criminalization of drugs and large-scale arrests for low-level offenders are two of the most important mechanisms sustaining the epidemic of mass incarceration. In practical terms these policies result in millions of individuals being brought into the criminal justice system at a young age. Typically drug offenses are linked to stop-and-frisk or profiling strategies that also target so-called quality-of-life arrests (turnstile jumping, loitering, disorderly conduct) as well as drug possession and small-scale sales (mostly involving marijuana).[11] Today there are over 14 million U.S. arrests annually for all offenses, but the largest single category of arrests is for nonviolent (and victimless) drug offenses—a total of 1.7 million arrests in 2008—of which more than 50 percent were for marijuana.

The focus on marijuana has been especially evident in New York City, where more than 353,000 people were arrested and jailed simply for possessing small amounts of marijuana between 1997 and 2006, as reported by sociologist Harry G. Levine and attor-

ney Deborah Peterson Small in their 2008 report for the New York
Civil Liberties Union, *The Marijuana Arrest Crusade*. In Levine's
September 2009 update, he pointed out the period 1997–2008 saw
"twelve times more marijuana arrests than in the previous twelve
years," even as marijuana use and availability in the city remained
largely unchanged.[12] In 2010, the New York City Police Department arrested 50,383 for misdemeanor marijuana possession, at a
cost of over $75 million: more marijuana arrests in that year alone
than in the nineteen-year period from 1978 to 1996.[13] This record-
high 2010 figure, reported the *New York Times* City Room blog,
"adds up to 140 arrests a day, making marijuana possession the
leading reason for arrest in the city."[14] The vast majority of these
arrests are of young people under thirty, and nearly 86 percent of
those arrested are black or Latino, even though research in New
York City and elsewhere in the United States consistently shows
that young whites use marijuana at higher rates.[15] The Drug Policy
Alliance's announcement of the 2010 marijuana arrest numbers
led the blog Gothamist to dub New York "the marijuana arrest
capital of the world."[16]

California, however, where the rightward-leaning midterm
elections of November 2010 saw the loss of a referendum to decriminalize and tax marijuana, offers the best data on racial im-
balance in drug enforcement. In June 2010 the California NAACP
announced its support for the California marijuana legalization
initiative—the first NAACP chapter to criticize racially biased
marijuana possession arrests. The California NAACP's report,
*Targeting Blacks for Marijuana: Possession Arrests of African Ameri-
cans in California, 2004–08*, clearly shows that young blacks use
marijuana at *lower* rates than young whites. Yet, in every one of the
25 largest counties in California, blacks are arrested for marijuana
possession at double, triple, or even quadruple the rate of whites,
and these misdemeanor marijuana possession arrests create criminal drug arrest records with serious consequences for the young
people targeted.[17] Beyond these racial disparities, which have been

the signature of the war on drugs in so many areas, we are now seeing the use of drug war tactics we associate with inner cities deployed against an even wider population.

As the number of marijuana arrests has grown (despite many reductions in the legal penalties for marijuana) enforcement and policing tactics have become harsher, taking on some of the characteristics of campaigns against hard drugs—such as the campaign in Tulia. Indeed, as drug markets (for hard drugs as well as for marijuana) are now developing in small cities and towns across the nation, the most punitive drug policing practices (so well known in the urban ghettos) are extending to the heartland of white America.

From Texas to the Berkshires

Great Barrington, Massachusetts, is a prosperous resort community of about 2,500 that functions as a tourism haven for well-heeled residents of New York and Boston. It is hard to imagine a place more different from Tulia, Texas, yet the same policing tactics that drove the mass arrests in Tulia were recently applied in Great Barrington, an example of the way that policing tactics in the war on drugs are migrating to new segments of the country.

Alcoholism had long been a problem in Great Barrington, accompanied by a very big AA community with many weekly meetings of the town's residents, who all knew each other very well. And there was plenty of pot smoking, going back to the older hippies who had tried to live off the grid in the surrounding area in the 1960s and '70s. More recently the drug problems of the outside world surfaced in the Berkshires—along with punk music, skateboards, pink hair, and goth styles—as local kids and students (mostly white) began to hang out downtown.

Inevitably the kids became a nuisance to the local merchants, who tried (unsuccessfully) to prevent them from lounging on the steps and smoking cigarettes in front of the increasingly posh clothing stores, antique shops, and pricey restaurants. Soon the kids gravitated to the more open spaces of the central parking area in back of the stores. Appeals by local merchants for these kids to stop loitering (and now sometimes smoking pot) were largely ignored by local law enforcement.

So it was a shock when, in the summer of 2005, a group of fourteen teenage kids were arrested for possession of and conspiracy to sell marijuana, swept up in a coordinated drug bust following eight months of work by the county and state drug task force—spearheaded by Berkshire County district attorney David Capeless. In Great Barrington, as in Tulia, a young undercover police officer had insinuated his way into the youth network of, in this case, primarily white, working-class kids, who had grown up together and were about to graduate from the local high school. He was befriended by a few of the kids and began to ask them to get him drugs as a favor—"just a couple of joints to get him through the weekend," because his girlfriend had dumped him. Over a few months he succeeded in getting several to oblige, and paid them for the drugs—perhaps even used them with the kids at parties.

Naive and easy to ensnare, these kids are considered low-hanging fruit by aggressive drug prosecutors. It is easy to make points with local voters concerned about the "drug problem," but not as easy to differentiate pot from harder drugs. Indeed, Capeless had been unable to significantly impact the more serious drug use and trade in pills and harder drugs that was already evident in nearby Pittsfield, the county seat, in the wake of the loss of twenty thousand jobs at a local GE plant between 1960 and 1980. Pittsfield also had a significantly poorer black and (more recently) Latino population, which had already seen a few drug overdoses and showed evidence of the presence of heroin and cocaine dealing in town.

Great Barrington's "drug problem," by contrast, seemed limited to the marijuana use in the parking lot. But the DA's approach to drug enforcement in Great Barrington shows what happens when strategies from the war against large-scale drug markets are deployed against low-level marijuana offenses on the part of teenagers. Because the parking lot where the kids sold joints to the undercover agent was within a thousand feet of an old schoolhouse and a day care center/nursery school (though the actual school is nowhere in sight of the lot), DA Capeless could invoke the threat of an additional charge for selling drugs in a "school zone"—in some cases two or three charges per individual, each of which carries a mandatory two-year prison sentence. The mandatory sentences are used as a tool by the prosecution to extract information about suppliers and larger-scale dealers—who are sometimes (but not usually) also students at the schools. Recent research at the Boston University School of Public Health shows that such use of school-zone drug laws (originally meant to protect children from drugs when they attend schools) has no effect on drug use at and around schools. That's because most kids use, buy, and sell drugs close to where they live, which in many communities means within 1,000 feet of a school. So, not surprisingly, the study found that 80 percent of *all* drug busts fall within such school zones.

However, the study also found that elsewhere in Massachusetts most local police exercise judgment in charging school-zone violations, and most prosecutors "break down" or dispense with these charges in first-offender cases. But not so in the Great Barrington case, where DA Capeless insisted on these charges and the mandatory prison terms they imply. Ironically, while this case was still active, the state legislature of Massachusetts voted to remove criminal penalties for marijuana possession of one ounce or less, replacing these with a $100 fine and no risk of imprisonment. While devoting all these law enforcement assets to entrap a few high school kids smoking pot in the parking lot, the more serious threat of hard drugs such as heroin, cocaine, amphetamines, and diverted pharmaceutical opiates (which are now widely available in many small cities and towns, in some cases more easily than marijuana) went unattended, with the lethal result of rising overdose fatalities in Western Massachusetts. (The first heroin overdose death I am aware of in Great Barrington occurred in the spring of 2010.)

These drug war battles, with their mindless punitiveness and mistaken focus, are part of what is driving the growing movement to decriminalize marijuana. Such efforts occur on a state-by-state basis—often by referenda or new laws allowing the therapeutic use of marijuana or "medical marijuana" programs. Despite strong resistance to these new local policies by federal authorities (especially under the Bush presidencies), in the last decade there has been significant movement toward reform of marijuana laws in the United States. In California over 250,000 individuals now have access to medical marijuana, and thirteen other states and Washington, D.C., have passed similar laws enabling individuals to use marijuana therapeutically. Each year this movement is extending to new states. The newly elected Republican governor of New Jersey is considering the legal growing of marijuana (under state control) to supply the medical marijuana dispensaries that passed a state ballot initiative last year, and Oakland, California, has proposed to do the same.

The story from Great Barrington makes clear that despite trends to reduce incarceration, the continued drive to criminalize and arrest drug users is not limited to places such as the Bronx or Tulia, Texas. With millions arrested and incarcerated for drugs in the big cities, the ideas and behaviors that characterize mass incarceration have now reached well beyond the mean streets of Mott Haven or Harlem. Following continued pressure to stop the spread of drug use across America (and the continued lack of adequate support for public health and therapeutic tools that could actually do that), the epidemic of incarceration has now spread beyond the big cities to the heart of small town America.

Stepping-Stones to Prison

While marijuana has often been called the gateway or stepping-stone to harder drugs, in fact it is marijuana *arrests* that are the stepping-stones to prison. A common pattern over the last three decades has been for minor drug offenses (most often for marijuana) to mark the initiation of a criminal record, future arrests, and eventual imprisonment. In New York State, the number of people imprisoned in state penitentiaries for nonviolent drug offenses (mostly possession and small-scale sales of drugs) between 1980 and 2008 grew from 1,500 to 20,000—rising from about 12 percent to 30 percent of all incarcerations in this period.[18] As drug use and drug dealing expanded throughout the 1980s and 1990s to become the central economic element of life for many poor communities (and especially for reentering prisoners), the prison population grew. Federal, state, and local agencies (who share responsibility for enforcing the nation's drug laws) report that in 2007 over 1.8 million state and local arrests were made for drug abuse violations in the United States, up from fewer than 700,000 in 1982—an increase of over 50 percent in the drug arrest rate nationally, taking the population growth over that time into account.

High rates of exposure to the criminal justice system for adolescent boys and young men is now the norm in many inner-city communities of color. Half of those arrested are twelve to twenty-six years of age, a group accounting for less than 20 percent of the U.S. population. In the United States in 2005 alone, over 2 million young men between the ages of 16 and 24 were arrested and exposed to the workings of the criminal justice system. About 50 percent of those who have these early encounters with the criminal justice system will go on to have further arrests and serve time not just for continued low-level offenses (especially drugs) but also for more serious crimes later in life, as they are increasingly exposed to the criminal justice system and its adult offenders. The effects of that exposure are not trivial. The experiences of arrest and brief custody while being "processed" by the police, the corrections system, and the courts can be very damaging for the already shaky lives of so many young people.

Furthermore, along with the increase in arrests came an increase in incarceration that also does not seem to correspond to an increase in actual crime. As social scientist Glenn Loury writes in his book *Race, Incarceration, and American Values*, between 1980 and 2001 about 50 percent of complaints resulted in an arrest, but the probability that an arrest would result in imprisonment more than doubled, from 13 percent to 28 percent.[19] While the number of prisoners incarcerated for violent crimes tripled in this period even as violent crime reached historically low rates, most significant for epidemic mass incarceration is that imprisonment for the far more numerous nonviolent offenses tripled as well. And for drug offenses (also nonviolent), the increase in arrests was elevenfold.

As Loury notes, this increase in arrests and imprisonments, accompanied by longer sentences, even as crime has dropped, is a sign of our society becoming "progressively more punitive . . . because we have made a collective decision to increase the rate of punishment," especially for blacks.[20]

Figure 7.2. Percentage of U.S. Males Likely to Go to Prison by Age and Race/Ethnicity

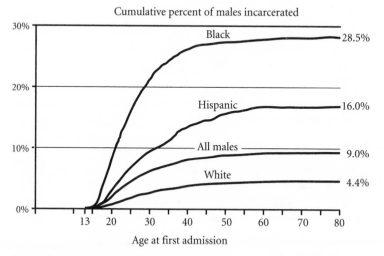

Source: Thomas P. Bonczar and Allen J. Beck, "Lifetime Likelihood of Going to State or Federal Prison," Bureau of Justice Statistics, March 1997, NCJ 160092, http://bjs.ojp .usdoj.gov/content/pub/pdf/Llgsfp.pdf.

This is no abstraction. We could readily see in Figure 7.1 (page 82) how this probability has changed dramatically since the 1970s in the direction of increased punitiveness. Figure 7.2 shows the relationship of race/ethnicity to a standard measure of punishment in the United States: the lifetime probability of men going to prison. In Figure 7.3, for the ages 16–26, we see the early beginning of the cycle of imprisonment that leads to these huge lifetime rates. This is especially true for black males, where the likelihood of going to prison for the first time is six- to eightfold that of white males at every age.

Figure 7.3. Chances of Going to State or Federal Prison by Age, Gender, and Race/Ethnicity

| | Cumulative percentage of resident population expected to go to state or federal prison for the first time, by age | | | | | |
	25	35	45	55	65	Lifetime
Total	2.4%	4.0%	4.7%	5.0%	5.1%	5.1%
Sex						
Male	4.3%	7.0%	8.2%	8.7%	9.0%	9.0%
Female	.3	.8	1.0	1.0	1.1	1.1
Race/Hispanic origin						
White*	.9%	1.7%	2.1%	2.4%	2.5%	2.5%
Male	1.7	3.0	3.7	4.1	4.3	4.4
Female	.2	.4	.5	.5	.5	.5
Black*	8.4%	13.6%	15.4%	15.8%	16.0%	16.2%
Male	15.9	24.6	27.4	28.0	28.3	28.5
Female	1.1	2.7	3.3	3.5	3.6	3.6
Hispanic	3.6%	6.3%	8.2%	9.1%	9.4%	9.4%
Male	6.3	10.7	13.9	15.4	15.9	15.9
Female	.4	.9	1.3	1.5	1.5	1.5

*Excludes persons of Hispanic origin.

Note: The cumulative percents represent the chances of being admitted to state or federal prison for the first time, by age. Estimates were obtained by sequentially applying age-specific first-incarceration rates and mortality rates for each group to a hypothetical population of 100,000 births.

Source: Thomas P. Bonczar and Allen J. Beck, "Lifetime Likelihood of Going to State or Federal Prison," Bureau of Justice Statistics, March 1997, NCJ 160092, http://bjs.ojp.usdoj.gov/content/pub/pdf/Llgsfp.pdf.

In a recent study, "Minor Charges, Serious Consequences: The Collateral Damage of Misdemeanor Arrest," research psychologist

Ricardo Barreras studied more than two hundred individuals who were arraigned in Bronx Criminal Court in 2008 after being arrested for nonviolent misdemeanors—mostly drugs and quality-of-life crimes such as trespassing, loitering, or jumping turnstiles in the subway. He found that almost 50 percent of the sample experienced "increased stress or burdens resulting from the arrests," along with evidence of more long-term negative impacts, including loss of work and/or income (17 percent), serious gaps in health care (missed medical appointments or medications) or disruption of education (14 percent), and negative impacts on already precarious housing (11 percent).[21]

These impacts of frequent arrests and even brief periods of detention are of course added to the persistent social and economic problems already prevalent in the lives of the poorest, most marginal populations. This negative impact extends to the health and emotional well-being of their family members as well. In the Bronx, repercussions often include crises around immigration for the 25 percent of Bronx cases who are not citizens. For this population, an arrest for even a single marijuana joint, jumping a turnstile, loitering on the front steps of one's own building, or talking back to a cop can send a person to Rikers Island, New York City's central receiving lockup and detention jail, which admits over 100,000 arrestees per year. One of the most serious implications of being remanded to Rikers is that the city jail is where U.S. Immigration and Customs Enforcement (ICE) profilers and screeners await. ICE uses fingerprints, computer databases, and interviews to scrutinize the large populations of Hispanics, Haitians, and other foreign-born individuals who come through Rikers, looking for any "irregularities" in their immigration status. Those with irregularities are further detained—often without any recourse to legal services, and with immediate deportation an ever-present possibility. Even green card holders, in this country legally and awaiting citizenship, under some circumstances can lose their green cards for arrests associated with minor offenses.

The introduction of drug war policing tactics into schools also plays an important role in perpetuating the epidemic of mass incarceration, particularly among minority youth. The New York Civil Liberties Union (NYCLU) has a program called School to Prison Pipeline aimed at reducing the high rate of criminal justice involvement of those New Yorkers most vulnerable to this system—young black and Hispanic males. The program focuses in particular on addressing the pernicious role that school safety programs now play in early initiation to the criminal justice system, including exposure to police, arrest, and jail as the result of infractions formerly thought to be best handled by school principals.

Angela Jones, a young educator and community organizer for the New York Civil Liberties Union, tells this story of Anthony, one of the many young black men who faced early, wholly avoidable exposure to the full force of the criminal justice system.

> Anthony is a sixteen-year-old African American student, raised in a low-income family in New York City. In middle school he received multiple suspensions for disruptive behavior and was identified as having behavioral and learning disabilities. Anthony was one of about 100,000 New York adolescents who attend a school with permanent metal detectors; every day he went to school, Anthony was asked to take off his belt and put his book bag through a scanner. But one recent Friday, hoping to make weekend plans with his father, Anthony had his cell phone in his pocket. The metal in the cell phone set off the detector and he was forced to surrender it to school safety agents. Angry that his cell phone had been taken and unsure how he'd connect with his father, he couldn't concentrate on the lesson in class and was reprimanded by his teacher for not doing his work. Anthony, increasingly upset, talked back to his teacher and was asked to leave the classroom and go to the dean's office, which he refused to do. The teacher

called a school safety agent (a uniformed New York police employee), who came into the classroom to escort Anthony to the dean's office. Anthony refused to go with him. The school safety agent yanked Anthony out of his chair. Anthony was enraged and pushed the safety agent away.

This scenario can easily be understood within the scope of ordinary male adolescent psychology as the result of adults needlessly escalating a struggle about authority into a full-blown confrontation. But in this instance, Anthony's behavior is addressed within the model of policing and arrest that was designed for dealing with potentially dangerous criminals. The techniques of control and punishment used here mimic the enforcement style of the adult criminal justice system. Any high school teacher in America would understand the things that need to be done to "chill" the situation described above—deescalating it to a quiet talk with an educational or psychological professional to hear Anthony's side of the story, and some positive action to help him connect with his father. But this is no longer about school or a teen's frustrations. The metal detectors signify our bloated, overextended system of crime and punishment that has seeped down to the schools and is epitomized by the permanent presence of metal detectors in about half of all New York City public schools. Anthony's story continues:

> The safety agent proceeds to handcuff Anthony in front of his classmates and arrests him for assault. He is then taken to the local police precinct, where he waits to be processed by the police. Anthony's mother arrives and is told that he won't be able to see a judge today—it is Friday afternoon and they have all left for the day. He will have to spend the weekend in a detention center.
>
> Anthony is released from the detention center on Monday and goes back to school, only to find that he's been suspended for one year for assaulting a school official and is required to attend an alternative learning center—full of

other students who have also been suspended. When Anthony petitions to return to his old school, the petition is granted, but he is behind in his studies and in danger of failing. A school guidance counselor informs him that he has the option of a GED, which Anthony accepts. But GED courses do not take his learning disabilities into consideration, and the process takes longer than expected. Without the GED he cannot find work nor contribute to his family's support.

By now Anthony is spending time with other older youth, also not in school, who sell drugs. He is soon arrested for possession and sent to a juvenile facility for two years. When Anthony is released, he is no closer to obtaining his GED and is too old to attend a transfer school. He has no marketable skills and now also faces the stigma faced by any formerly incarcerated person. Feeling lost and suffering from depression, Anthony begins to use hard drugs. Anthony is arrested once again for possession of a controlled substance with intent to distribute. This is his second offense, and under the state's Rockefeller drug laws he is sentenced to nine years in prison.

The story of Anthony that we have seen unfold is no longer about a teenage boy and his school. Instead it rapidly morphs into a narrative about law enforcement—a tale of policing, arrest, detention, and, all too soon, drugs, crime, and incarceration—a prime example of the school-to-prison pipeline in action.

The advent and growth of this school-to-prison pipeline did not correspond with an increase in school violence—indeed, crimes against and by youth were actually declining before school-based zero tolerance policies were instituted.[22] But the enforcement apparatus of zero tolerance policies in schools by uniformed school safety personnel (5,200 in New York City alone) are designed to feed the pipeline. As funds are diverted from more effective school counseling, mental health services, and after-school programs (all cut to the bone by the budget shortfalls of the 2008 recession), schools turn to police models and begin to rely on more punitive approaches: suspension, expulsion, citations, summonses, and arrests.

These methods are borrowed wholesale from the drug war tactics and policing methods of the adult criminal justice system and are now installed in many U.S. schools, along with metal detectors. Once in place, they soon become the default approach to handling an ever-expanding list of disciplinary problems—including bringing cell phones and MP3 players to school, smoking cigarettes, and skipping class. Criminal charges are brought against youth in schools for violations that never would be considered criminal if committed by an adult. As the NYCLU program description puts it, "Students who might easily be disciplined through a visit to the principal's office end up in jail cells—this is the essence of the Pipeline." Suspensions in school now serve the same function as drug arrests do in the adult community—a source of initial infections that perpetuate the intergenerational transmission of mass incarceration. This juvenile justice system, linked to family courts, is seemingly designed to prepare these children for a future in adult prison. Often this cycle of ever-deepening involvement in the criminal justice system is initiated within the juvenile justice system, now the subject of increasingly shocking disclosures of abuse and inadequate professional care of troubled kids.[23] This system is a huge toxic exposure to children from the very families and communities that have already borne the brunt of prior mass incarceration policies affecting their parents.

The concept of a school-to-prison pipeline highlights the key role this mechanism plays in the inception of sharp racial disparities that have come to characterize the adult system.[24] According to data compiled by the NYCLU, zero tolerance school policies and suspensions disproportionately affect students of color and those with learning disabilities. In 2000, black students represented 17 percent of national public school enrollment but accounted for 34 percent of suspensions; special education students represented

8.6 percent of public school students but 32 percent of youth in juvenile detention nationwide. Black students with learning disabilities are three times more likely to be suspended than white students with learning disabilities, and four times more likely to end up in correctional facilities. School disciplinary, juvenile, and criminal records also work against disadvantaged students when they apply for colleges, scholarships, jobs, and selective high schools. In many places, having a criminal record can prevent students and their families from living in public housing.

It is critical to realize that increases in the use of arrest, jail, and imprisonment as the default punishment for an ever-widening set of nonviolent offenses is, in effect, a policy that leads to long-term imprisonment of an ever larger population of young males—especially black men. The epidemiology of the collective impact of this is apparent with each successive year of age. Arrest starts young, usually in adolescence—especially for males. Beginning at age fifteen, the likelihood of going to prison grows regularly up to age twenty-five, after which the chance of getting arrested for the first time and going to prison declines rapidly. But once these youths are involved in the criminal justice system, their lifetime probability of continued involvement with recurrent arrests and incarceration grows apace.

As the overall U.S. rate of imprisonment for adults climbed from around 100 per 100,000 in 1975 to over 500 per 100,000 in 2005—a 425 percent increase—a profound change also took place in the scale and significance of mass incarceration for the young members of the same high-impact feeder communities where incarcerated adults live. Figure 7.4 illustrates the probability of a twenty-year-old black male in America being in prison. It provides the numbers and rates of twenty-year-old black men in U.S. prisons for the years between 1974 and 2004, when this population grew from under 4,000 in 1974 to more than 11,000 by 2004—from 1.5 percent to 4.7 percent of all the twenty-year-old black males in the United States.[25]

Figure 7.4. The Increasing Proportion of Twenty-Year-Old Black Males in Prison in the United States, 1974–2004

Year	Number of 20-year-old black men*	Number of 20-year-old black men in prison	Percentage of 20-year-old black men in prison
1974	256,852	3,922	1.5
1979	278,738	6,200	2.2
1991	291,874	9,463	3.2
2004	250,000 (est.)	11,859	4.7

* From U.S. Census data.

These data reflect a threefold increase in the likelihood of a twenty-year-old black male being imprisoned in the years between 1974 and 2004—a consequence of increased drug arrests and increasingly harsh sentencing practices.

Source: U.S. Census and Bureau of Justice Statistics data, based on unpublished studies of the age of U.S. prison populations by M. Brittner.

Later "enhancements" of the risk for exposure to the criminal justice system, such as the amped-up penalties of the "crack laws." (The notorious hundredfold discrepancy between the penalties for crack and powder cocaine was recently reduced by a new federal law, but a first offense of possessing one ounce of crack still calls for a mandatory five-year sentence.)[26] These types of harsh drug sentences and the increases in denial of parole have resulted in ever-longer sentences that are now being served in full.[27] Strict rules about probation, parole, and repeat offenses have also led to increased rates of recidivism and rearrest—the factors that also serve to give mass incarceration its self-perpetuating features. Because so many drug arrests are of young men who have not yet established themselves in working adult lives, this level of drug law enforcement combined with long sentences has proven especially disruptive. The data show that destabilizing individual lives during this phase of development makes recovery from drugs more difficult and the chances of finding gainful employment and secure family and housing arrangements subsequent to imprisonment almost zero.

The age, race, and gender that predict risk of exposure—

young, black, male—also combine with social and economic class and educational and vocational disadvantage—to doom criminal justice system entrants to remain trapped in the system. The white middle-class drug user, even if arrested with drugs, is far more likely to have legal counsel, to be able to make bail, and to avoid jail time. His family typically has more resources to make bail and provide a home, and he likely has a social and family network that helps him get jobs and access to education. White middle-class youth arrested for drugs are more likely to get probation and to go to counseling or drug treatment, while black teens go to juvenile detention centers that are the nurseries for future prison careers. These minority youth are initiated into the criminal justice system early and in large numbers. The longer sentences of the mandatory drug penalties and the recidivism that is so common allow ample time and opportunity to form or solidify relationships in prison based on criminal networks involving gangs or dealing drugs that carry over to the community after release. Long sentences, often far from home, also erode prosocial family and community relationships on the outside.

In places outside the United States, the damaging possibilities of youth arrest and early incarceration, as well as age and first-offense status are factored into official criminal justice policies.[28] Thus in British Columbia, Canada, probation officers deliberately avoid placing younger first offenders together with older inmates with multiple offenses. This is designed to keep younger drug offenders from being drawn into criminal networks in the communities from which prisoners come and to which they return. These networks transcend the prisons and are preserved as social networks in the communities, accounting for the admission (and readmissions) of so many prisoners. Furthermore, in Canada there are few mandatory sentences to launch the long criminal careers we see in the United States, although conservative Prime Minister Stephen Harper has pushed since 2010 for mandatory drug sentences in Canada.

The relationship of drug laws to crime and public safety remains complex. U.S. crime rates climbed from the early 1970s to 1993—the first twenty years of the war on drugs—but have gone down since 1993, only to begin to rise again in 2008. This recent rise is especially true in many smaller cities that are now experiencing the same sort of growth in gangs and drug markets that larger, older cities saw in the 1980s. Overall the evidence indicates that each birth cohort reaching adolescence since the start of the war on drugs in the 1970s has been more and more likely to spend time in prison. The recursive pattern that ensues can be seen within a public health model as "reinfection" or relapse in the medical sense, establishing a pattern of chronicity in the individual that keeps him within the pale of the epidemic far beyond his initial prison term.

Parental Incarceration and Intergenerational Transmission

For the New York City feeder communities that account for the majority of imprisonments in New York State, we know that in 1970 the probability of any child having a parent go to prison was 2–4 percent. Today that figure is 25–30 percent.[29] With this in mind, we can easily understand that a very high prevalence of incarceration goes beyond individual effects and becomes a transformative force in the lives of entire communities.

The wholesale imprisonment of young men and women, 52 percent of whom are parents, has created a generation of "children of the incarcerated"—the second major reason mass incarceration has become self-sustaining. Over half of these parents (44 percent of men and 83 percent of women) either lived with or had regular contact with their children at the time of arrest and incarceration. Their children therefore grow up without access to at least one parent for about 50 percent of their childhoods.[30] These children are statistically at extremely high risk of themselves becoming prisoners later in life. Estimates are that between one-third and one-half of all juvenile hall inmates have a parent who has been incarcerated.[31] One 1992 study showed a 29.6 percent delinquency rate for children of incarcerated parents and a 22.2 percent rate of gang affiliation.[32] This pattern of parental involvement in the criminal justice system is strongly associated with prisoners' children's subsequent arrest as juveniles, and predicts time spent in juvenile detention facilities. Because of these associations, the study of parental incarceration is now under way in earnest for the first time, with large-scale research on both the epidemiological and psychological effects of parental incarceration being conducted in the United States.[33]

In a recent paper entitled "Parental Imprisonment, the Prison Boom, and the Concentration of Childhood Disadvantage," Yale sociologist Christopher Wildeman examines "how imprisonment transforms the life-course of disadvantaged black men."[34] Using census data, life tables, and U.S. prison surveys to examine trends and racial disparities associated with these phenomena, Wildeman estimates the risk of parental imprisonment by age fourteen for black and white children born in the years 1978 and 1990 (i.e., children born at the beginning and at the end of the most explosive period in the growth of incarceration in the United States). He also estimates the risk of parental imprisonment as a function of educational attainment of the parents, focusing on high school dropouts.

Wildeman's results dramatically demonstrate the consequences of both the growth of parental incarceration and the widening inequalities of blacks and whites, as the adult rate of incarceration has grown over the last thirty years. His data are compelling: more than one in seven black children born in 1978 (14 percent) had a parent imprisoned during their childhood, versus one in forty white children (2.5 percent) born in 1978. For children born in 1990, the rates grew worse, and the disparity continued: one in four black children (25 percent) versus one in twenty-five white children (4 percent) had a parent imprisoned during their childhood.

Further, Wildeman shows that "inequality in the risk of parental imprisonment between white children of college-educated parents and all other children is growing . . . as a distinctively American childhood risk." By age fourteen, 50.5 percent of black children born in 1990 to high school dropouts had a father imprisoned.

Mass Incarceration as Criminogenic

The Norwegian criminologist Nils Christie asked of punishment, "When is enough enough?" Is there a tipping point for the use of incarceration, the effects of which are visible in the communities most affected? Mass incarceration, concentrated as it is in specific communities, may alter the social ecology of these neighborhoods—often irreparably—and this is the third major reason that mass incarceration is self-perpetuating.[35] As more and more residents of neighborhoods targeted in the war on drugs are arrested, these levels of incarceration begin to damage the social fabric that typically keeps individuals functioning as law-abiding citizens—family, church, and neighborhood social support networks. These forms of social capital typically sustain the fabric of communal support that is especially important in the poorest communities, which are exactly the ones most heavily impacted by mass incarceration.[36]

When imprisonment (seen at first as individual sentences for individual crimes) is inflicted at such a scale, there is now some indication that it actually becomes criminogenic—that is, mass incarceration may work to create new criminals. Earlier studies of New York by Columbia criminology researcher Jeffrey Fagan with Valerie West and Jan Holland show that imprisonment rates are highest in New York City's poorest neighborhoods. "Although not necessarily the neighborhoods with the highest overall crime rates [these] also show the perverse effects of incarceration on crime rates . . . such that over time higher incarceration rates predict higher crime rates one year later." They also show that "the growth of incarceration and its persistence over time are attributed primarily to two factors: drug enforcement and structured sentencing laws that mandate imprisonment for repeat felons." They point out that these neighborhoods with high rates of incarceration invite closer and more punitive police enforcement and parole surveillance, contributing to the growing number of repeat admissions and "the resilience of incarceration even as crime rates fall." [37] This is one of the first studies detecting this "perverse effect" of more punitive sentencing policies and enforcement on crime rates, but more have followed, finding similar results.

Sociologists Todd Clear and Dina A. Rose have also examined this counterintuitive idea—that, on a local basis, more punishment may lead to more crime by damaging family and social networks in ways that diminish their positive capabilities. Clear and Rose are among the growing number of criminology researchers who are now building a body of empirical research that looks at this problem directly. Clear and Rose's research was conducted in the Tallahassee area of Florida and looked at crime rates in the years following the surge of arrests and imprisonments in that area, one community at a time. Crime rates—especially drug offenses—actually increased despite mass arrests in these communities in the previous period. Very high rates of imprisonment concentrated in specific communities cause social disorganization, undermining the normal social controls of family and community that are the best (and most natural) guarantors of good behavior. [38]

In the Clear and Rose model, mass incarceration diminishes social capital—the social web of local community relationships, connections, and accountabilities that defines healthy communities. When social capital is lost, the quality of social support diminishes as well, including trust and communication among neighbors, access to help with the children, emergency cash, or a place to sleep when you've been burned out of your home.

The recognition (and measurement) of the negative effects on communities of high incarceration rates is important. In some societies, where drug use has been uncoupled from prosecution and arrest as public policy, this chain of transmission of risk can be interrupted. For example, marijuana can be made available through legal coffee shop outlets, as it is (most famously) in the Netherlands and now elsewhere in Europe and in some parts of Australia.[39] In America for the last 35 years, however, our choice of mass arrests and imprisonment has effectively been the agent of a spreading disease far more serious than drug use—creating huge increases in an ever-enlarging population at risk of exposure to imprisonment.[40] Low-level drug arrests and the exposure to the virulent criminal justice system in the United States act to "infect" individual hosts by weakening their links to prosocial elements of family and community (i.e., reserves of social capital found in families and social support networks) and exposing them to anti-social elements and the criminogenic effects of the criminal justice system. In Canada, there is a conscious effort to incorporate these lessons into a system that is averse to the overincarceration so common in the United States. So far these models have successfully reduced recidivism but are still struggling with the primary issue of drug dependency in the treatment-deprived environment that exists even in Canada, especially for mental health services.[41]

The drug laws and their massive enforcement system constitute the environment that has promoted the greatest increases in exposure to incarceration among those who are most susceptible to arrest and conviction. Most often (in 95 percent of U.S. drug arrests) this is via plea bargains among drug users who have been caught with drugs or entrapped by street enforcement teams in buy-and-bust operations. This leads to their arrest, incarceration (for brief periods at first), and later to "persistent offender" status, as their involvement in the criminal justice system becomes chronic, with frequent arrests and periods of reincarceration. A criminal justice system whose response to a wide range of crimes relies almost entirely on incarceration as its default mode of punishment thus takes on self-perpetuating features.

8

CHRONIC INCAPACITATION: THE LONG TAIL OF MASS INCARCERATION

The effects of being incarcerated stay with individuals and their loved ones long after a prison sentence is over. In this respect, individuals exposed to mass incarceration often develop the kind of long-term disabilities and limitations of functioning characteristic of other epidemics of chronic illnesses, such as heart disease or diabetes. The impact of the poor physical and mental health of many prisoners as they enter the system, and the deplorable conditions in many prisons, combine with a set of "invisible punishments" that continue to stigmatize and disadvantage former prisoners once they have returned to their communities.[1] These enduring effects of punishment (its long tail) play at least as large a role in determining future well-being and life prospects for former prisoners as do the effects of prison time itself.

Ideas about the impact that imprisonment has upon individuals and populations are at the core of all theories of criminology. Typically, the focus is on the role of incarceration as a means of controlling crime. Conventional wisdom in criminology is that the purpose of incarceration is to deter crimes in two ways. One is through the example of punishment of offenders, to build the fear of punishment by others who are caught committing a crime. The other intended role of imprisonment is incapacitation, the goal being to remove the individual from society for some length of time, thereby limiting his or her ability to commit new crimes while behind bars.[2]

While the literature of criminology is full of studies debating the effectiveness of incarceration as a deterrent (something that is very difficult to prove or disprove), there is a general consensus about the role of incarceration in incapacitation. By removing offenders from society, the argument goes, we limit the harms they might do while free. By this logic, the greater the number of criminals who are incarcerated (and rearrested for violations of parole or for new offenses), the more crime is prevented overall—at the very least by the incapacitation effect. This is a common claim used to support high imprisonment rates and long sentences (without parole) as the best guarantor of public safety.

This argument has intuitive appeal. But the data on the incapacitation effects of mass incarceration are often equivocal, in part because so many other factors determine the variations in crime rates in any society, and because most of those exposed to the effects of incarceration return to the community.[3] Nonetheless, the large drop in major crimes we saw in the United States between 1993 and 2003 (rising again now in many parts of the country) is often attributed to the effects of the two decades of large-scale imprisonment that accompanied it. But there is abundant evidence that incapacitation by incarceration plays only a restricted role in lowering crime: criminologists now attribute a maximum of 25 percent of the U.S. crime drop to incapacitation by imprisonment. Most suggest a much lower figure of 5–10 percent.[4]

Other important social changes have been advanced to account for the remaining 75–95 percent of the crime drop, including demographic changes associated with a declining birth rate due to availability of birth control and abortions beginning in the 1970s, that reduced the size of the population at highest risk for commission of crime: young black and Hispanic males from single-parent homes.[5] The economic gains of the 1990s also offered many more opportunities for entry-level jobs in urban communities. This period also saw the stabilization of many of the illicit drug markets in the largest urban centers in the United States, reducing much of the street violence associated with drug dealing. But the crime drop is also used to claim the "success" of aggressive policing tactics employing racial profiling, stop-and-frisk tactics, and the use of loitering and trespassing misdemeanor charges that yield many arrests but few criminal arraignments, convictions, or sentences, while spreading anger and antagonism toward law enforcement among minority youth.[6]

Yet the notion persists that by taking criminals off the street, imprisonment prevents them from committing new crimes, and remains a cornerstone of the justification for high rates of imprisonment. This simple idea—getting the "bad guys" off the street—has a strong intuitive appeal, aside from satisfying some more retributive impulses.

What we have not acknowledged, however, are the long-term consequences of mass incarceration. The lifelong debilitating effects of exposure to the criminal justice system and incarceration produce a set of consequences that incapacitate these individuals in quite another way, making them far less able to return to productive life once their prison term ends. This is the long tail of incarceration, incapacitating individuals for their life after release from prison. This form of personal incapacitation imposes a set of permanent impediments to full reintegration to society, essentially functioning as a chronic disability throughout the course of the ex-prisoner's life. This view of incapacitation (as an imposed disability on life outside of prison) is a radical alternative to the common claims (largely unsupported by evidence) of the rehabilitation of individuals or of the societal benefits of incarceration as a preventive measure against crime.

Further, except in the most extreme cases, the concept of lifelong incapacitation by imprisonment is fundamentally anathema to our laws and our criminal justice system's sense of proportionate punishment. The United States is still a nation with a strong belief in the possibilities of redemption. Moreover, there is the overwhelming reality that even with millions of protracted prison sentences in effect, most prisoners eventually emerge from confinement and reenter the communities from which they came. In 2009, 700,000 former prisoners reentered American society. In theory, these prisoners have paid their debts to society by imprisonment for a set period of time, determined by the length of their individual prison sentences. This includes periods of parole, representing that portion of a prison sentence served in the community under restrictive supervision. In parole, we have tacitly agreed to an ongoing form of incapacitation that is still significantly restrictive but much less expensive than a prison sentence.

We earlier used the public health measure of potential years of life lost to incarceration (YLL) as a different way to understand the most elemental impact and vast scale of incarceration in America. We saw that all those years of life lost to imprisonment are comparable to the figures for many other great epidemics and man-made disasters. There is another related public health concept that allows us to quantify and understand the impact of mass incarceration on America. This concept views incapacitation as a disability and measures its magnitude in our nation's population.

Most health problems (and most epidemics) do not lead immediately to fatalities; more often they are associated with long-term disabilities and chronic illnesses resulting in serious restrictions in the ability to function in the everyday world of home, family, community, work, and school. Disabilities can restrict the ability to walk, to talk, to think straight, or to breathe. In terms of public health, incapacitation amounts to a form of disability, and often disability is the most meaningful way to understand the damaging individual and population effects of the most common traditional diseases of the heart, lungs, and nervous system. Years of good health lost are known as disability-adjusted life years, or DALYs, defined by the World Health Organization as "the sum of years of productive life lost due to disability" and are a measure of the "burden of disease."[7] One DALY is equal to one year of healthy life impeded, and the concept is a powerful way to understand how various illnesses impact a population's health. For example, a 1990

WHO report indicated that five of the ten leading causes of disability were psychiatric and neurological conditions, which account for 28 percent of all years lived with disability but only 1.4 percent of all deaths and 1.1 percent of years of life lost.[8] Psychiatric disorders are traditionally not regarded as a major epidemiological problem, but using a DALY calculation shows that they have a huge impact on populations. The concept of DALY is far better suited than YLL or mortality rate to understanding the many long-term consequences of chronic diseases that limit our ability to work productively and to live fully as normal citizens and family members.

Both parole and probation often impose restrictions that severely limit an individual's ability to work, travel, and effectively reunite with family and social networks. Thus we can see the years of "softer" community control (by parole or probation) as years that impose a more limited sort of disability. Using DALY, we can also evaluate the impact of imprisonment and its aftermath upon the individuals released from prison in a given year, measuring the functional incapacitation (or disability) that is associated with the extension of criminal justice controls into the home community. These limitations affect, for example, the ability to get work, obtain decent housing, apply for social benefits, and restore family and social ties. For the United States as a whole in 2004, for instance, there were 12,844 DALY per 100,000 in the general population, meaning that, at any time, about 13 percent of the population was disabled due to the usual problems of illness and aging. Of the 700,000 individuals released from prisons in 2009, about 30 percent were sufficiently "disabled" to fail at reentry and were reincarcerated in the first year after their release, yielding a DALY rate of 30,000 per 100,000 (or 30 percent). Thus the DALY figure due to incarceration is more than double that due to all other disabilities in the general population.

Statistics aside, we can all relate to disability in our own and our family's lives—periods when we cannot care for ourselves or fully participate in everyday life as independent adults. And all those who have had severe or long-lasting physical disabilities (especially as children) know the pain and often the stigma that come with them. When the effects of incarceration extend over a lifetime, as they do for millions, the consequences of massive exposure to the criminal justice system must also be understood as a major determinant of lifelong disabilities. These disabilities affect the physical and mental health of those populations subject to the highest rates of imprisonment—the poor, and ethnic and racial minorities—effectively incapacitating or handicapping them for life in the community. From a public health perspective, many of the damages imposed on individuals by the criminal justice system produce or sustain a number of long-term disabilities. Incarceration systematically damages key elements of the psychological and physical health of prison inmates, causing or exacerbating conditions including addiction, mental illness, and chronic infectious or metabolic diseases. Restrictions placed on ex-felons after they have left prison, including restrictions on access to employment, housing, public benefits, and civic participation, as well as the stigma of being an ex-felon, disable their ability to function effectively in the outside world, incapacitating their attempts to regain a foothold in noncriminal life and to reestablish a place in their families and home communities.

The consequences of involvement with the criminal justice system can now be viewed as the long-term effects of a toxic exposure. While a primary intent of incarceration is to punish by depriving the prisoner of the benefits of freedom for a finite period of time, the effects of incarceration on long-term physical and mental health serve to extend punishment far beyond the period of the sentence itself. What has never been publicly debated, but what seems to have emerged as a result of our current draconian incarceration policies, is a situation where millions of Americans are essentially permanently excluded from normal life, largely because of their extended or exceptionally harsh exposure to the criminal justice system. Viewed in these terms, mass incarceration imposes the same burden for our society as many chronic diseases associated with occupational hazards (for example, coal, asbestos, or nuclear radiation), the physical and emotional trauma of war, or the deprivations of severe poverty and family disintegration.

It is impossible to reconcile this situation with the basic rights granted to each of us in the Constitution. Yet every year, hundreds of thousands of prisoners become afflicted with physical and mental diseases in prison that do not go away at the end of their sentences, and have their lives disabled by the punitive ways our society treats ex-felons. Recognizing that the vast majority of those who enter this system do so as non-violent offenders (who then become progressively more damaged as they are exposed to the criminal justice system), helps us to understand mass incarceration as a man-made disaster of epidemic scale. The next sections explore these effects in two distinct realms: during incarceration itself, and in postrelease life.

Disabilities Imposed by Time Spent Within Prisons

Prison is not meant to be pleasant; that's why it's called punishment. But neither is it meant to be "cruel and unusual."[9] None of the rationales for imprisonment in the United States includes acceptance of the concept that this form of punishment, most of it for low-level crimes, should cause long-term hardship or permanent harm to individuals and their families. While some societies still defend the most lurid responses to crimes (including flogging, amputations, stoning, and executions), most developed Western democracies show a long and clear trend away from those sorts of punishments. In developed nations (formerly including the United States) there has been a steady movement since World War II toward better prison conditions, shorter prison sentences, and more genuine and effective efforts at rehabilitation.

In part this has come about as a result of recognition of the eventual reentry of most prisoners into the communities from which they came. In the United States, of the 700,000 prisoners who now leave prison each year, over 60 percent return directly to their home communities. Most are seeking to reestablish the family and social ties that constitute their only social capital—the networks of support so necessary to the prospect of their resuming normal lives. But most do not stay outside very long: recidivism is massive, with about one-third of released prisoners rearrested within the first twelve months, and two-thirds of released prisoners returning within three years.[10] This is the most powerful factor that now defines incarceration as a chronic condition—the "revolving prison door" that has become the hallmark of America's brand of mass incarceration.

The conditions within prisons have powerful effects, many of which stay with the individual for life. The adverse effects of incarceration on individual prisoners include the ongoing consequences of poor health care services in prisons; failure of prison security to provide a safe environment (the ensuing rape, violence, and gang activity that have become a routine part of prison life); serious and persistent mental health problems and inadequate mental health care in prisons; and a paucity of addiction treatment and the absence of effective drug rehabilitation. All this is in addition to the immediate and longer-term psychological implications of trauma associated with overcrowding, poor prison conditions, and many severe disciplinary methods, including isolation and solitary confinement.

Health

To be fair, the serious health problems so prevalent among the populations most likely to be incarcerated do not begin with arrest and imprisonment. Overwhelmingly, prisoners come from poor minority communities; and their ills in prison faithfully mirror those that these same populations suffer at home. Drug addiction and alcoholism, infectious diseases—especially sexually transmitted diseases—viral hepatitis, and HIV/AIDS are at very high levels in this population and demand significant care in prison as well.

Ironically, imprisonment is often the occasion for these individuals to receive medical care for the first time—prisoners are the only civilian population in America with a right to health care. Under the Eighth Amendment, which bars "cruel and unusual punishment," prisoners have a unique constitutional entitlement to decent medical care. But, despite frequent court mandates to provide this care, extremely poor inmate health services persist in many of the nation's prison systems.

Many of the chronic illnesses seen in prisoners—addiction, mental illnesses, diabetes, hypertension, asthma, heart disease—were poorly controlled at the time of admission to the prison system as a result of poverty and long histories of poor access to health care. In some cases, such as those involving court-ordered care for prisoners with HIV/AIDS, for example, prisoners may receive better medical care in prison than they would receive outside. But the norm is inadequate health care for the incarcerated.[11] This tends to worsen the preexisting condition, especially in the case of addiction and mental illness, which figure so prominently in the reasons for arrest and incarceration in the first place. More than 80 percent of U.S. prison inmates enter prison with histories of or current problems with drug abuse or dependency, and drug use often continues throughout prison stays—typically at lower levels, but often with more dangerous practices associated with clandestine injecting via unsterile needles and syringes shared by many inmates.[12] Drug users are generally distrusted when it comes to receiving routine medical care (both in prisons and outside), with many medical providers discounting their demands for pain medications—even in cases involving bone fractures.

Health care services are a constant flash point for correctional institutions in America. According to a recent study of New York State prison health services by the Correctional Association of New York, based on prison visits and reviews of the formal grievance process, medical care is the "most highly grieved issue in most state prison systems," representing about 20 percent of all complaints filed by inmates.[13]

The issues representing the greatest percentage of medical grievances are:

- Denials of and delays in access to health care
- Inadequate examinations by nurses and physicians
- Failures to treat chronic medical problems expeditiously
- Delays in access to specialists and inadequate follow-up by prison providers on specialists' recommendations
- Problems with receiving medications and the health education needed to comply with complex medication regimens

In addition to the neglect of preexisting medical conditions and major lapses in consistent medical care, the deprivations and stresses of prison life and the poor quality of prison diet increase the severity of chronic diseases.[14]

The care of HIV-infected inmates is a major issue (and expense) in the prisons of states with high rates of AIDS. Thus New York State (with over 53,000 prisoners in 2010) has about 1,700 HIV-infected inmates receiving medical care using antiretroviral drugs, at an annual cost of more than $25 million. But best estimates are that these 1,700 are only about one-third of New York State prisoners infected with HIV—most of whom do not know they are infected (there is no routine testing of inmates). These HIV-positive individuals have a great need for testing programs to identify them and to initiate their treatment as early as possible—both for their own benefit and for reducing transmission risk in the prison and, on reentry, in their communities.

Women's health care needs, always more prominent than those of young males, are also inadequately addressed in prisons. In addition to facing all the routine gynecological, reproductive, and nutritional issues of women who are not incarcerated, the overwhelming majority of women in prisons are survivors of violence and trauma.[15] And more than 60 percent of incarcerated women are parents, who must deal as best they can with separation from their children and families, along with the depression, anxiety, and low self-esteem that this entails. Not surprisingly, incarcerated women suffer from serious mental illnesses at much higher rates than male inmates.[16]

Increased potential for contracting an infectious disease such as AIDS, hepatitis, TB, or a sexually transmitted disease (STD) is another feature of prison life. Inmates face a heightened risk of acquiring bloodborne infectious diseases, due in large part to the sharing of contraband drug injecting equipment with others in prison. The risk of acquiring STDs is increased through consensual but unprotected sex, and by rape in prison. An estimated 60,500 inmates—4.5 percent of the nation's prisoners—report experiencing sexual violence ranging from unwanted touching to nonconsensual sex, according to a recent Bureau of Justice Statistics survey of federal and state inmates.[17]

Yet few inmates see any point in seeking the protection of prison authorities; a separate Bureau of Justice Statistics survey found that only about 6,500 official allegations of prison sexual violence (by staff or inmates) were reported to correctional officials in 2006—about 11 percent of the cases. The report found that "low response rates from victims are due to embarrassment or fear of reprisal, challenges in verifying victims' self-reports, and lack of common terminology to describe sexual abuse."[18] Recent reports of sexual offenses by staff in juvenile detention centers have launched a new federal investigation of sexual violence faced by close to 3 million juveniles arrested each year.[19]

Adult inmates are regularly transferred from one prison to another, with disruptive effects on any health care that they do get. Prisoners often assert (and a recent New York study confirms) that they are not promptly seen and evaluated when transferred to a new facility. Records often fail to follow them in a timely fashion. Many inmates being discharged from custody leave without adequate documentation of their medical status and without appropriate medication or a medical discharge plan.[20]

Another effect of mass incarceration and longer sentences is that prison inmates are now an aging population. According to the most recent report of federal Bureau of Justice Statistics, 4.3 percent of all inmates in the United States in state or federal prisons were over the age of fifty-five as of midyear 2008, compared with 3.5 percent at midyear 2004, a 23 percent increase. It costs $70,000 per year to house older prisoners, two to three times the cost of housing younger prisoners.[21] In 2006, 5 percent of California's inmate population was over the age of fifty-five, but that population accounted for 22 percent of the off-site hospital admission costs the state saw that year. This situation will only worsen in the years to come as longer sentences intersect with shorter life expectancies. As previously noted, many of today's prison inmates will die in prison because their sentences exceed their life expectancies. Of the 5,200 men at Louisiana's infamous Angola penitentiary, an 18,000-acre former plantation, journalist Mary Foster estimates that "about 90% will die there because of the length of their sentences, and many will be buried in the bleak Point Lookout Cemetery on the grounds."[22]

These health issues collectively mean that, even for those who enter prison young and healthy, a prison sentence is tantamount to being afflicted with a chronic illness or long-term disability. The deplorable state of prison health care is one of the prime reasons a prison term leads to a lifetime of full or partial incapacitation, transforming a finite sentence of incarceration into a lifelong disabling condition.

Drug Addiction and Its Treatment in Prison

Significant problems with drug use and alcoholism are ubiquitous in prisons. Federal studies estimate that 60 to 83 percent of the nation's correctional population has used drugs at some point in their lives, twice the estimated drug use of the total U.S. population (40 percent).[23] Drug offenders accounted for 21 percent of the state prison population in 1998 (up from 6 percent in 1980), 59 percent of the federal prison population in 1998 (up from 25 percent in 1980), and 26 percent of all jail inmates, mirroring the steady increase in arrests for drug offenses over this period. Women in state prisons were more likely than men to report using drugs in the month before their offense (62 percent versus 56 percent) and were also more likely than male inmates to have committed their offense under the influence of drugs or while engaging in petty theft or prostitution to get cash for drugs.

Many other countries now offer a wide range of treatments (including methadone) to incarcerated drug users and seek to avoid imprisonment for those with addictions.[24] But most U.S. prisons have been resistant to this approach. While there are many very dedicated peer drug counselors in prisons, their efforts to rebuild self-esteem and equip inmates to deal with the dependency and high risk of relapse are thwarted in these anti-therapeutic environments dominated by punishment. There is little incentive to offer effective drug treatment in modern American prisons—a neglect framed as part of the prison ideology in which inmates must assume "personal responsibility" for their present circumstances. Building on this seemingly reasonable conception, most drug treatment in prisons is moralistic in tone, depicting addiction as evidence of personal weakness (confirmed by the great personal failure that incarceration has come to represent) and often seen by inmates themselves as ample justification for their current punishment.

In consequence, the way we treat drug addiction in prison has become an extension of the moral crusades of America's war on drugs—an exercise in the mystification of what drug use means, confounded with a strong dose of guilt and blame, rather than a less judgmental health approach. Legitimate questions of how best to minimize the harm from drugs are subordinated to the goals of zero tolerance—even for therapeutic drugs that soften the pains of withdrawal. Drug problems of prisoners have now become the basis of a virulent ideology of condemnation and demonization, undermining any personal strengths they may bring with them into prison and creating further, lifelong problems for inmates— problems that may result in their rapid return to drug use after release.

Evidence for this failure can be seen in the high rates of drug overdose that occur in the period immediately following discharge of drug users from prisons. Multiple studies have confirmed that overdose deaths among people who used heroin prior to incarceration are increased tenfold in the two weeks after release from prison, as compared to the usual overdose rate.[25] This result has been seen in the United Kingdom, Canada, and Australia, which all have drug problems similar to that in the United States but incarceration rates of drug users that are only about one-quarter of our own.[26] Opiate overdoses are thought to be due to the loss of tolerance associated with the greatly reduced level of use of opiates in prison. In the United States, the most significant reason for this can be found in the failure to treat opiate dependency adequately in prisons. More specifically, it can be attributed to the failure to allow known opiate-dependent individuals to use methadone in prisons. When there *is* drug treatment (consisting mostly of prisoners talking in groups), the most common philosophy is modeled after the drug-free therapeutic communities that philosophically dominate American drug treatment—generally to the exclusion of approaches that employ medications such as methadone or buprenorphine, known to be the most effective methods available to treat opiate addiction.

The high rate of drug incarcerations ensures that drug problems will be very common in prison populations. State corrections officials estimate that between 70 percent and 85 percent of inmates need some level of substance abuse treatment. But sustained, professional, supervised drug and alcohol treatment is currently available in fewer than half of federal, state, and local adult detention facilities. Juvenile correctional facilities are also staffed to serve only a fraction of those who need treatment services. In approximately 7,600 correctional facilities surveyed, 172,851 inmates were in drug treatment programs in 1997, less than 11 percent of the inmate population and less than 20 percent of those with addiction histories.[27]

While some state prison systems expanded drug treatment programs in the 1990s, these have now been cut severely in most systems—another consequence of the recent state budget crises including, for example, a 40 percent reduction in California in 2009 alone.[28]

The injection of heroin within correctional facilities has been documented in many prisons worldwide and continues to exist, notwithstanding vigorous attempts to deter and detect the importation of drugs and injecting equipment into these facilities.[29] Although episodes of drug injecting inside these facilities are generally far less frequent than in the community, adverse consequences (including HIV infection) are well documented. While the use of methadone or buprenorphine maintenance for addiction treatment is prohibited in state and federal prisons throughout the United States, a small number of local jails do offer brief detoxification programs using these medications. In the past decade, some jail facilities have begun to offer methadone maintenance treatment as well. A large-scale methadone maintenance treatment program, serving two thousand patients per year, was established in New York City's Rikers Island jail in the 1970s—operated by the Montefiore health service—the first jail program to offer this treatment in the United States. The Rikers Island approach continued methadone for all new admissions already in maintenance at the time of arrest (mostly detainees) and initiated methadone treatment for those with sentences of less than a year. This program paved the way for several small pilot methadone programs in prisons and jails in Maryland, Puerto Rico, and New Mexico. But all such programs face formidable struggles to maintain their modest gains in the face of widespread correctional hostility to this approach to drug treatment, despite the powerful evidence of its benefits elsewhere in the world.

By contrast, as of January 2008, methadone maintenance has been implemented in prisons in at least twenty-nine other countries or territories, with the proportion of all prisoners in care ranging from less than 1 percent to over 14 percent.[30] In Canada, any methadone maintenance patient who is incarcerated is maintained on methadone throughout his or her time in custody, and many heroin users are started on methadone during a period of federal incarceration. Even in Eastern Europe and Central Asia, some prisons now offer methadone maintenance or a short course of methadone-to-detoxification in some pretrial detention facilities.

A program recently instituted in Baltimore provided methadone maintenance for prisoners who were soon to be transferred to community-based methadone programs at release. These prisoners had significantly better outcomes than a control population provided only "counseling and passive referral" after discharge. Results included more time spent in treatment during the twelve-month postrelease period, and far fewer positive urine tests for heroin and cocaine.[31] But because of hostility toward the use of methadone in correctional settings in the United States (it is also barred in almost all drug courts), such programs are rare. Accordingly, the first thing many released prisoners do on getting out is seek relief by injecting heroin—often with lethal results. Over 25 percent of drug fatalities due to overdose are now thought to stem from this phenomenon.[32] The failure to address addictions in the criminal justice system is the single most significant reason for rearrest and recidivism once released. This amounts to a systemic failure that diminishes each individual's chances of successful reentry at the end of a prison term. Instead, reentry becomes associated with a resumption of drug use that, while not altogether absent, had been greatly reduced during imprisonment. This is a clear case of incarceration heightening a disabling condition with lethal effects on the outside.

AIDS and Incarceration

Coming full circle to our earlier discussion of AIDS, there is now growing evidence that mass incarceration is driving the continued incidence of HIV in the United States. In 2008, the CDC estimated that approximately 56,300 people were newly infected with HIV annually—up 20 percent from previous estimates.[33] While constituting 12 percent of the U.S. population, African Americans account for 45 percent of all new AIDS diagnoses and are now estimated to have an incidence rate eight times that of whites. For African American women, the magnitude of these racial disparities is even more pronounced—their HIV rates are nearly twenty-three times the rate for white women.[34]

Discovering the causes of such dramatic disparities in HIV rates is a very high public health priority and crucial for efforts to control the U.S. AIDS epidemic. Although a great deal of research already exists on racial and ethnic disparities in HIV, much of it remains focused on individual risk behaviors while neglecting more collective phenomena, including effects related to involvement with the criminal justice system.[35]

But the association of incarceration and the AIDS epidemic is now very strong. According to research published by public health experts, between 17 and 25 percent of all people in the United States who are estimated to be infected with HIV disease will pass through a correctional facility each year, roughly 190,000 to 250,000 of the country's estimated total of 1 million HIV-positive individuals.[36] Research on HIV risk is now examining the social conditions and structure of this group's community networks, especially within African American populations. Focusing on the role of the criminal justice system as an important factor driving the AIDS epidemic, these data suggest a strong correlation between the circumstances of high arrest and incarceration rates and high HIV prevalence within many African American subpopulations and their communities.[37] HIV rates among African Americans in New York state prisons are estimated at 5–7 percent among men and 7–9 percent among women, and the risk appears to carry over to their sexual partners in their home communities.[38]

Recent evidence also suggests that cyclical patterns of release and reincarceration may foster instability in sexual and social networks involving drug use, leading to broader social disorganization that increases AIDS transmission risk. In conjunction with unstable housing, untreated drug addiction, and recurrent imprisonment, a "churn" in social networks occurs that is now typical of these communities. These destabilizing effects act within the social networks established in the prison feeder communities of many cities to produce increases in risk for HIV transmission both by sex and by drug use. Two-thirds of prisoners return to incarceration within three years of release and subsequently reenter their home communities a few years later. This pattern of serial disruption spreads risk across these communities, affecting even those not directly linked to ex-prisoners. "Risk networks" can include drug use and sexual partners of ex-prisoners, who may form a bridge between this population's periodic exposure to the criminal justice system and the surrounding population. This connection between the widespread incarceration of African American males and high rates of HIV in many urban communities dramatically demonstrates an important long-term community health impact of the criminal justice system—part of its development as a chronic condition.

Mental Health

Mental health problems are another hallmark of U.S. prison populations and another source of the mounting toll of lifelong disabilities that incarceration imposes. Following the deinstitutionalization from psychiatric hospitals of the chronically mentally ill from the 1950s through the 1970s, the strong association of drug use, addiction, and mental illness led the U.S. criminal justice system to become the default response for these former hospital patients—most dramatically among the poor and homeless.

University of Chicago law and criminology professor Bernard Harcourt notes that a growing number of individuals "who used to be tracked for mental health treatment are now getting a one-way ticket to jail." Pointing to a Justice Department study released in September 2006, Harcourt notes that 56 percent of those in state prisons (and a higher proportion of those in local jails) reported mental health problems within the past year. He states that one reason for the increase in the number of mentally ill inmates may be a trend away from institutionalizing these individuals in mental hospitals and asylums. He writes, "Though troubling, none of

Figure 8.1. Institutionalization in the United States per 100,000 Adults, 1928–2000

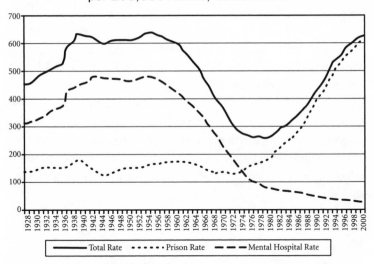

This figure illustrates the shift of institutionalization in America in the twentieth century from mental institutions to penal institutions. The closing of 75 percent of psychiatric hospitals in the 1950s and 1960s (associated with the rising use of new psychiatric medications) led directly to an increasing number of prisons to house many of the populations formerly confined in mental hospitals.

Source: Bernard Harcourt, Public Law and Legal Theory Working Paper No. 227, 2006 University of Chicago.

this should come as a surprise. Over the past 40 years, the United States dismantled a colossal mental health complex and rebuilt— bed by bed—an enormous prison." Today, 400,000 to 600,000 prison inmates (15–20 percent of all prisoners) have a major acute or chronic psychiatric disorder, and serious psychiatric cases are now recurrent in the prison system.[39]

In addition to failing to treat many preexisting mental health problems experienced by prisoners, incarceration itself, and especially many of the most punitive practices employed to control prisoners, often creates new mental health issues, including the long-term posttraumatic effects of rape, violence, and humiliation—effects that stay with and handicap individuals long past the end of their prison sentences.

Homicide and Suicide in Prisons and Jails

In the most extreme cases, the experience of prison or jail leads to homicide or suicide. Paradoxically, in some ways prisons are safer than many of the communities from which so many inmates come: during 2002, the homicide rate in state prisons was 4 per 100,000, and in local jails 3 per 100,000, versus 6 per 100,000 in the general, nonincarcerated population. On the other hand, the rate of suicide in state prisons (14 per 100,000) is statistically significantly higher than in the general U.S. resident population (11 per 100,000). In local jails, the suicide rate is over four times higher (47 per 100,000) than outside. These data provide very concrete evidence that the particular stresses associated with the harrowing process of arrest, police handling at booking and arraignment, and pretrial confinement—and even brief detention in chaotic and crowded jails—are particularly traumatic, and can often prove fatal. Over 40 percent of those in solitary confinement, a widely used disciplinary measure, develop major psychiatric disorders. Not surprisingly, while those placed in solitary represent only 5 percent of the prison population, they account for almost half of the suicides.[40]

The Use and Impacts of Solitary Confinement

In 2009, Harvard surgeon Atul Gawande published a startling article in the *New Yorker* about the use of solitary confinement in American prisons. The title of the article, "Hellhole," evokes an image of carceral barbarism—of men placed in pits in the blazing prison yard of the 1957 film *Bridge on the River Kwai*. But Gawande's piece (which appeared under the banner "Annals of Human Rights") raises a more disturbing issue for Americans: with only 5 percent of the world's population (and 25 percent of its prisoners), the United States now has over half of all the world's prisoners who are in long-term solitary confinement.[41]

More than 25,000 inmates are permanently in isolation in supermax prisons, where they may spend years locked in small, often windowless cells with solid steel doors, let out for showers and solitary exercise in a small, enclosed space once or twice each week. A report by Human Rights Watch found that supermax prisoners have almost no access to educational or recreational activities and are usually handcuffed, shackled, and escorted by two or three correctional officers every time they leave their cells.[42]

Supermax prisons were ostensibly designed to house the most violent or dangerous inmates, but many of the prisoners there do not meet these criteria. Instead, supermax prisons are a response to the rapid growth of prison populations and shrunken state budgets, which have overwhelmed the ability of corrections professionals to operate safe, secure, and humane facilities. Lacking funds to recruit, properly train and retain adequate staff, or to provide programs and productive activities for those in existing congregate prisons, these thinly staffed, overcrowded, and impoverished facilities breed more tension and violence.

An additional 50,000 to 80,000 prisoners are housed in "restrictive segregation units," many of them in isolation. In other kinds of prisons, the trend toward more long-term solitary confinement is inseparable from the period of explosive growth of mass incarceration. Gawande notes, "The wide-scale use of isolation is, almost exclusively, a phenomenon of the past twenty years."[43] Indeed, sustained isolation has now become institutionalized as a cornerstone of our nation's criminal justice system and its requirement for extreme sanctions to handle the mass of prisoners.

In 1995 a California federal court reviewed the state's first supermax prison, noting that the conditions "hover on the edge of what is humanly tolerable for those with normal resilience." As a physician, Gawande immediately recognizes the impact on these individuals' psychiatric conditions, citing an 1890 observation by a Supreme Court inquiry that noted the effects of isolation: "a considerable number of the prisoners fell, after even a short confinement, into a semi-fatuous condition, from which it was next to impossible to arouse them, and others became violently insane; others, still, committed suicide; while those who stood the ordeal better were not generally reformed, and in most cases did not recover sufficient mental activity to be of any subsequent service to the community." Clearly the practice of locking away tens of thousands of prisoners in solitary confinement for long stretches of time has a profoundly deleterious effect on the long-term mental health of these inmates.

Life on the Outside: Chronic Incapacitation After Prison

There is now wider recognition that populations who are temporarily incapacitated by confinement will still spend the most significant portion of their remaining lives outside prisons. *But They All Come Home*, the title of the 2005 book by Jeremy Travis, former head of the National Institute of Justice, reminds us of this crucial reality. This is not necessarily a smooth transition, as former New York State prisoner Elaine Bartlett concluded in Jennifer Gonnerman's powerful book *Life on the Outside*, "My sentence began the day I was released."[44]

Research seldom systematically considers the many incapacitating effects of criminal justice involvement after release and the way these reduce the chances of former prisoners' successful reentry and adaptation to life on the outside. Having once been removed from their communities by force, most reentering prisoners want to reconstitute their lives and repair the damaged ties to loved ones. However, even with their prison sentences served (or forestalled by parole), most ex-prisoners must now deal with another set of punishments that constitute a less visible but very powerful web of new restrictions—forms of social incapacitation that raise many obstacles to their successful reintegration to their communities and effectively block their chances of a better life outside of prison.

In addition to the well-known restrictions placed on individuals on parole (curfews, drug tests, rules of association, etc.), a less well-known set of what has been termed "invisible punishments" often affect the entire life span of formerly incarcerated individuals.[45] Most states maintain rules that frequently bar many categories of ex-prisoners from living in public housing, from working in a wide variety of jobs and professions, and from receiving a range of forms of public assistance including school subsidies, income support, and food stamps. These rules also bar many ex-felons from serving on juries and from voting, even after they have been released and have completed parole. Having served their formal sentences, ex-prisoners will endure new forms of punishments capable of generating more anger, more shame, and the scars of permanent social stigma.

In the public health model we have considered here, we may see this as a form of chronic incapacitation. Exposure to the system disables an individual's basic abilities to compete in our society and to assume a productive and responsible place in it. Ex-felons in America today are incapacitated just as surely as in those societies that cut off thieves' hands or blind them. These enduring disabilities, so often culminating in rearrest and reincarceration, are a basic engine that makes mass incarceration into a chronic condition.

Housing and Homelessness

One of the most important ways in which incarceration affects prisoners and their families is by placing many formal and informal limitations on obtaining stable housing, especially for those with drug convictions. Of course, many young men and women who go to prison come from unstable households to begin with (often due to their own parents' and family members' previous involvement in the criminal justice system). Recent research also indicates that male imprisonment promotes subsequent homelessness of their offspring.[46] While little known to people who have not experienced them, restrictions on access to public housing for many ex-felons create a huge barrier to successful reentry for those whose formal prison sentences have ended. Of the ways a criminal record diminishes an ex-prisoner's ability to obtain and utilize public benefits, restrictions on access to publicly funded housing programs are among the most incapacitating for populations coming out of prison, and among the most aggressively enforced.

In addition to these formal rules, different public housing complexes have adopted their own restrictive policies regarding ex-felons. For example, a tenant newsletter distributed to the twenty thousand residents of the Grant Houses in Harlem in 2006 lists the names and addresses (and sometimes photos) of "undesirables"—previous tenants who have recently been convicted of felonies. Tenants are warned that these former neighbors are not allowed in the housing complex. Not only are they barred from living in the public housing where many were raised; ex-prisoners may not even visit without fear of being reported as "trespassers" and made subject to prosecution—a violation of parole that can get them thrown back in jail. Furthermore, such transgressions can even potentially jeopardize the leases of their own mothers or grandmothers, who are "guilty" of allowing ex-felons unauthorized access to public housing.

This banishment from the homes and communities in which they grew up affects almost all of the extended families of the

400,000 tenants of public housing in New York City—where perhaps 10 percent (40,000) are former drug felons, subject to these restrictions indefinitely, even after their formal sentences are finished. Although technically the means exist for allowing former prisoners to clear their names after a period of time, the specifics of what it takes to do so are very vague and seldom result in restoration of access to public housing benefits for former felons.[47]

Forced evictions are a prominent feature of these policies. In 1996, the federal government implemented the Housing Opportunity Program Extension Act, a "one-strike initiative" authorizing "local public housing authorities to obtain the criminal conviction histories and records from drug treatment facilities regarding the use of controlled substances of adult applicants for or tenants of public housing for screening and eviction purposes." In Oakland, California, the Public Housing Authority used this act to begin eviction proceedings against several elderly tenants whose family members, unbeknownst to the tenants, had been caught using drugs in or near public housing. Two of the tenants, Willie Lee and Barbara Hill, faced eviction from their homes after their grandsons were arrested for marijuana possession. Another tenant, Pearlie Rucker, faced eviction for her mentally disabled daughter's possession of cocaine three blocks from the Rucker residence, and for her adult son's possession of cocaine eight blocks away, though no drugs were found inside Rucker's residence. Another tenant facing eviction, Herman Walker, is seventy-five years old and disabled. Walker's "offense" was having an in-home caretaker who had been cited for narcotics and paraphernalia (Mr. Walker subsequently fired the caretaker).[48] The Rucker case came before the U.S. Supreme Court in 2002, which upheld this "one-strike policy" that evicts any public housing tenant whose family member or guest uses drugs within several blocks of the premises, regardless of whether or not the tenant was aware of the drug use.

A criminal conviction also limits a former prisoner's ability to get a home mortgage or to participate in Section 8 subsidized housing programs, although the rules on these restrictions are not clearly stated anywhere. The Internet is full of queries by former prisoners about this issue, sparked by the common experiences of former inmates and their inability to procure a mortgage. On one Web site, an attorney appealed directly to HUD for guidance: "The Department of Housing and Urban Development (HUD) administers the subsidized housing programs in most states. Someone I know was rejected due to 'unsatisfactory criminal history check,' among other reasons. Does the HUD subsidized housing program ban felons currently on supervision . . . ? If yes, PLEASE, if you have it, include a cite(s) to the statute, reg, admin rule or case law. Thanks in advance!"[49]

The housing restrictions facing former prisoners help create the chronic homelessness that is often a lifetime collateral consequence of imprisonment, with homelessness itself being a major risk factor for reincarceration. In a thirty-six-city survey, "prison release" was identified by officials as a major contributor to homelessness.[50] Recent studies in New York City reveal that more than 30 percent of single adults entering shelters under the Department of Homeless Services were recently released from city and state correctional institutions—a chronically disrupted group that continually cycles between incarceration and shelters. More than 10 percent of those coming in and out of prisons and jail are homeless in the months before their incarceration, which serves to increase their risk of homelessness upon reentry. For those with mental illness and those returning to major urban areas, the rates are even higher, about 20 percent.[51] University of Pennsylvania investigators Dennis Culhane and Stephen Metraux found that, among 48,424 persons released from New York State prisons to New York City between 1995 and 1998, 11 percent had entered a New York City homeless shelter within two years of release. This failure to assure housing after release from prison is associated with high rates of recidivism: 32.8 percent of the original study group released returned to prison in this same two-year period.[52]

A California study reported that while 10 percent of all the state's parolees were homeless, the rate was much higher—an estimated 30 percent to 50 percent—for those parolees living in large metropolitan areas such as San Francisco and Los Angeles. Conversely, the homeless or unstably housed population face very high risks for repeated incarceration: 49 percent of homeless adults reportedly spent five or more days in a city or county jail, and 18 percent had been incarcerated in a state or federal prison during periods of homelessness.[53]

Combining these factors produces some bizarre conjunctions. In 2007, Lareau J. Laube, a fifty-five-year-old Pennsylvania man and repeat sex offender, found himself unable to gain entry to a public shelter because of his criminal record. So he made an unusual request of Judge Stephen G. Baratta. After pleading guilty to giving a false name to police when arrested for sleeping at the library, Laube wanted to be given the maximum sentence. "I didn't have a place," Laube said. "I'm homeless." The judge sentenced Laube to six to twelve months and ordered that probation officials prepare a plan to ensure Laube would have a place to go after completing his sentence.[54]

Clearly, depriving those who have served their prison sentences of the right to access publicly funded housing creates an almost insurmountable disability as former prisoners attempt to rebuild their lives after prison.

Bars to Employment

In the economic climate following the 2008 recession and its subsequent high rates of unemployment, ex-prisoners face a daunting set of obstacles. The prospect of securing employment may be the biggest challenge of all. Even before the recession, many studies had shown the unemployment rates of formerly incarcerated people one year after release to be as high as 60 percent. In practice, formal restrictions on employment of ex-felons are now coupled with an increasing reluctance among employers to hire people with criminal histories, thus making even a brief prison sentence into a lifelong financial and social handicap.[55]

In addition to the prejudices and more formal restrictions on their ability to get jobs and take advantage of public programs supporting the poorest Americans, ex-prisoners are also subject to a complicated set of rules governing their ability to work in many trades and professions. In New York, as in other states, many jobs are closed to anyone with a prison record—from barbers and beauticians to physical therapists, real estate brokers, plumbers, and sanitation workers, all of which require state licenses that are predicated on applicants being "morally sound" individuals. New York State codes are typical of the scope of felony convictions' effects on trade, occupational, and professional licensing by states, which often stipulate that a person shall not be eligible to practice or engage in any trade, occupation, or profession for which a license, permit, or certificate is required if they have been convicted of a felony.[56] In New York State, over a hundred trades are covered by state licenses and so are denied to convicted felons. While petition to waive this restriction is possible, proving one's worthiness to state officials is a lengthy process and seldom successful. These rules, together with employers' general reluctance to hire former felons, mean that a conviction and prison term greatly diminish an individual's lifetime prospects for gainful employment.

A recent case illustrates this perverse pattern very well. Marc La Cloche spent his time in prison training to be a barber and was ready to apply his newfound skills to getting a job upon his release in 2001. But the Bronx native found himself facing a surreal situation when he applied for a barber's license: because of his felony conviction, his application was denied. Under state law, La Cloche could practice his trade—taught him by the state's Department of Corrections—only if he remained behind bars. An administrative law judge made an exception to the law and granted him a barber's license, but New York State appealed the decision, and the license was revoked. La Cloche died in 2008, never having obtained his license.[57]

Even employers willing to hire an ex-offender (perhaps with the benefit of a federal tax credit) are often prohibited by state law from doing so. While in some circumstances employers are forbidden to deny employment to someone simply because of a criminal record (unless there is a "direct relationship" between the crime and the prospective job), employment bans still extend across entire industries. For example, former prisoners are barred from jobs as vendors staffing food service operations in banking, loan, or financial corporations under other rules that do not allow former prisoners to work within "financial institutions"—even in the kitchens of these institutions.

Bars to Receiving Public Assistance

Federal statutes also bar access to public welfare funds for those with felony records, especially drug convictions. Ex-felons do not have access to federal programs of support for education, employment training, Section 8 housing, or food stamps. Because black males are most likely to experience criminal justice sanctions, they are also at far greater risk of facing the lifetime of social disadvantages that accompanies criminal punishment, which then helps maintain and exacerbate racial inequality.[58]

Food stamps are often the only benefit available to individuals or families who have maxed out their welfare income support under the Temporary Assistance to Needy Families (TANF) program and are most likely to be impoverished. Along with the many other forms of social and financial support withheld from ex-felons, denial of this particular benefit—literally taking food from the mouths of so many who need it—is a particularly cruel consequence of mass incarceration. Henrie M. Treadwell and Elisabeth Kingsbury, writing in the *Black Star News*, report, "Each year, hundreds of thousands of people released from U.S. prisons after felony drug convictions discover that serving time isn't their only punishment. They are permanently denied the life-sustaining benefits of food stamps and other public assistance. The restrictions come from the 1996 welfare reform legislation, which was adopted at a time when politicians in Washington were maneuvering to be perceived as tough on crime."[59] Texas, for example, has a lifetime ban on food stamps for people convicted of a drug felony—even though the state therefore loses out on federal funds that could be used to help people with drug felony convictions reestablish themselves as productive, lawful members of society. Without the support of federal food stamps, these people must rely on state, local, or privately funded services, which are now more limited than ever.

Civic Death: Felony Disenfranchisement and the Loss of the Right to Vote

Contrary to the foundations of democracy, 5.4 million Americans are denied the right to vote because of a felony conviction. Effectively, this means that millions of U.S. citizens have a profoundly diminished ability, if any at all, to influence the laws and policies that govern and devastatingly disrupt their lives. As International Criminal Court judge Albie Sachs has noted, in a democracy, voting is a fundamental "badge of dignity and personhood."[60] Most other Western democracies now allow inmates to vote while in prison. In Australia, where voting is legally mandated, a $100 fine is levied for *failure* to vote, even while in prison. But in the United States, disenfranchisement is a matter of state law for all but two states (Maine and Vermont) and Puerto Rico. Forty-eight states currently take away the right to vote for all imprisoned felons—some for their entire lifetimes. The basis of felony disenfranchisement in the United States is a core belief that those who violate the law should lose this right and benefit of citizenship, further underscored by the fact that in many states, convicted felons are also prohibited from serving on juries.

Amidst a voting system of hanging chads, defective electronic

voting machines, and archaic and cumbersome registration procedures, the machinery of felon disenfranchisement is the picture of
modernity and uncharacteristic efficiency. After a felony conviction, court records are sent to a prisoner's local board of elections,
and the prisoner's name is purged from the voting lists. Once removed from the voting rolls, ex-prisoners bear the burden of getting reinstated, with a wide range of unclear and generally poorly
understood rules governing reinstatement—in some states ex-
felons must show they are now "morally fit to vote," for example.
In Florida there is a backlog of three years' worth of applications
for restoration of individuals' right to vote.

The end of a prison sentence is not the end of disenfranchisement, for thirty-five states extend disenfranchisement to the period of parole. And thirty states exclude those on probation from
voting, which effectively doubles the number disenfranchised nationally. Indeed, 75 percent of disenfranchised felons are not in
prison.[61] Finally, in eleven states some or all are barred from voting
for life if they have ever had a felony conviction anywhere in the
United States. This prohibits one-quarter to one-third of all black
men in these states from voting.

The overall scale and impact of felony disenfranchisement is
wholly consistent with the chronic disabling effects of a felony
conviction and record. According to the Sentencing Project, which
tracks and tabulates the statutes and consequences of felon disenfranchisement laws and practices:

- An estimated 5.3 million Americans, or one in forty-one
  adults, have currently or permanently lost their voting
  rights as a result of a felony conviction.
- Among African American men, 1.4 million, or 13 percent, are disenfranchised, a rate seven times the national
  average.
- An estimated 676,730 women are currently ineligible to
  vote as a result of a felony conviction.

- Given current rates of incarceration, three in ten of the next generation of black men can expect to be disenfranchised at some point in their lifetime. In states that disenfranchise ex-offenders, as many as 40 percent of black men may permanently lose their right to vote.
- About 2.1 million disenfranchised persons are ex-offenders who have completed their sentences. The state of Florida had an estimated 960,000 ex-felons who were unable to vote in the 2004 presidential election.[62]

Serious efforts are under way to alter these old laws on a state-by-state basis. Each state has developed its own process of restoring voting rights to ex-offenders, but most of these restoration processes are so cumbersome that few ex-offenders are able to take advantage of them. Nine states that disenfranchise certain categories of ex-offenders are now permitting application for restoration of rights for specified offenses after a waiting period (e.g., five years in Delaware and Wyoming, two years in Nebraska). Even the two states (Florida and Virginia) that still indefinitely deny the right to vote to all individuals with felony convictions after they have completed their sentences have begun to open more pathways to voting.

In the meantime, however, felon disenfranchisement significantly diminishes the collective civic voice of young men of color, with important consequences for the functioning of American democracy.

In 1833, that astute observer of criminal justice in the United States, Alexis de Tocqueville, famously noted that most "individuals on whom the criminal law inflicts punishments have been unfortunate before they became guilty." Now we can also see that the histories of personal and social misfortunes that send individuals to prison in the first place persist well beyond their period of confinement, continuing to punish them, their families, and their communities for many years afterward. Criminal justice controls and their toxic aftermath are now endemic in all neighborhoods and families with high rates of imprisonment. In these communities, mass incarceration and chronic incapacitation sustain and reproduce themselves through the conversion of individual criminal sentences into lifelong chronic conditions that leave permanent scars psychologically, physically, and socially. The combination of harsh prison conditions, restrictive rules governing life after prison, and the chronic nature of many of the problems that led to incarceration in the first place (especially long-term drug and mental health problems) makes conviction for even a minor offense into a lifelong disability, one that individuals who have been imprisoned have little chance of overcoming in their lifetimes. In addition, the stigma of imprisonment can last a lifetime. A fifty-year-old grandmother who had served time in prison a decade earlier for a drug offense described the lingering suspicion and mistrust even within her own family years after her release from prison: "Visiting with family at my mother's house, my aunts still take their handbags with them when they leave the room I am in. . . . Once you've been in prison you can take ten thousand showers, but you never get the stench of it off you."

The enduring nature of many of these effects are consonant with neither our nation's rhetoric about fair and just sentencing, our general acceptance of the possibility of redemption, nor our constitutional prohibitions against cruel and unusual punishment. The long-term consequences of incarceration are invisible only to those who do not know someone who has been through the criminal justice system. For felons, ex-felons, their families, friends, and communities, the effects are all too visible, and each individual who comes into contact with our current system of mass incarceration remains damaged by it for life.

9

THE CONTAGION OF PUNISHMENT: COLLATERAL DAMAGE TO CHILDREN AND FAMILIES OF PRISONERS

The previous chapter described the ways that punishment by incarceration operates like a chronic disease to systematically incapacitate individuals, wounding them physically and psychologically while in prison and disabling them for a future of successful participation in American life. Mass imprisonment leaves a trail of psychological, social, and economic damage affecting entire populations where incarceration has become normative, creating a chronic condition affecting millions over a long span of time.

But this epidemic has another characteristic that causes an even larger population to be adversely affected in ways that also help to sustain the epidemic: mass incarceration is contagious. Borrowing from the vocabulary of modern warfare, the children, spouses, parents, siblings, and other family members of those who have been incarcerated are the collateral damage of our criminal justice policies. While blameless of any crime themselves, these innocent victims, particularly the children, also are psychologically wounded by mass incarceration. As we shall see, they too are significantly disadvantaged in their own lives by the far-reaching effects of our system of mass incarceration, just as surely as if they had been convicted and sentenced alongside their parents.

When we use an epidemiological lens to look at mass incarceration, we can see this epidemic's intergenerational, self-sustaining effects clearly. Many studies are now demonstrating that children with incarcerated parents are significantly more likely to become incarcerated themselves.[1] While it may have started as a mechanism for punishing legal transgressions by individuals, mass incarceration now damages everyone in each prisoner's orbit, most horrifyingly his or her children. Our punitive policies have effectively spawned a whole new generation who, as a result of a parent's incarceration, experience a host of disadvantages that become expressed as school failure, increased health and psychological problems, homelessness, and, ultimately, increased probability of being arrested and incarcerated themselves. Recognizing this problem, New York State moved to treat parental incarceration as a mitigating factor in termination of parental rights, passing legislation to allow "expanded discretion" on a case-by-case basis for those parents in prison or rehabilitation.

The collateral damage of mass incarceration can be observed in almost every prisoner's family. Prior to incarceration of a family member, these same families struggle with poverty, unemployment, low wages, and unstable housing. Imprisonment exacerbates each of these and adds a host of new hurdles for prisoners and their families.

Imprisonment puts a huge strain on many already shaky marriages and relationships. In New York and many other states, prisoners are often incarcerated more than a hundred miles from home in rural areas inaccessible to poor families from the city. Merely maintaining lines of communication while a spouse is incarcerated can present a major financial and logistical burden. Other costs associated with family members in prison include the cost of visiting the prison, paying for phone calls at inflated rates, and providing funds that allow inmates to buy amenities (soap, toothpaste, clean underwear)—all of which create new economic hardships for families already struggling in the absence of the earnings of the incarcerated member.[2] When loved ones do manage to visit, prison visiting rooms tend to be frightening and unwelcoming places, especially for children. These conditions mean that half of all families never visit at all.

The risk of divorce is high among men going to prison, reaching 50 percent within a few years after incarceration.[3] The marriage rate for men incarcerated in prisons and jails is lower than the American average. For blacks and Hispanics, it is lower still.[4] And many prisoners have fathered children with more than one partner, producing fragile families of unmarried parents and their children.[5] With a strong association between incarceration history and the instability of the parents' relationships from the time of their child's birth, unmarried couples in which the father has been incarcerated are 37 percent less likely to be married one year after the child's birth than similar couples in which the father has never been incarcerated.[6]

Even when a relationship has succeeded in overcoming the years-long strain of incarceration, reentry often imposes new burdens. During long periods of incarceration, the absence of the incarcerated parent forces families to restructure their lives. When the incarcerated parent returns, the family system must once again adjust, with many newly established roles and routines disrupted and new conflicts emerging, even if the parent returns from prison but does not live with the family.

Financial problems now loom large for many families in America, especially for reentering prisoners and their families. Few decent jobs (ones with good pay and benefits) are available to populations lacking high levels of education.[7] And most reentering men were in dire economic straits *before* going to jail or prison. Coming out, they are in significantly worsened condition, with little in educational or vocational advancement to show for the time spent in prison. After prison, they must deal with the stigma of a criminal record and the poor workplace attitudes that attend many jobs available to ex-felons. Crucially, the capacity (of a father especially) to serve as a provider and reestablish a measure of self-respect and respect from his children is often central to regaining a viable position within the family structure upon reentry. In addition, he will be expected to meet child support obligations, even when he does not reside with his family. In 2009, the majority of returning New York State prisoners (52 percent) were unemployed, and only 9 percent had full-time jobs at above minimum wage.[8]

A report published by the Osborne Association notes that the level of public funds dedicated to restoring economic stability for returning prisoners has been severely cut back in the current economic climate, undermining the ability of reentering parents to survive in the mainstream economy. The financial and emotional struggles of time apart and the hurdles of reentry mean that the effects of a prison term extend to all members of a prisoner's family.[9]

Social Engineering and Child Removal

Some of the most severe collateral consequences of a prison term fall on the families of prisoners who have children, including on the children themselves. Ironically, many disadvantages imposed on the families of prisoners with children occur under the rubric of government programs intended for child protection. Separation due to incarceration often leads to foster care placement and pressures for termination of parental rights under federal laws.

The federal Adoption and Safe Families Act (ASFA) was enacted in 1997 to "reduce the number of children in foster care and release them for adoption." The seemingly laudatory goal of this program (preventing children who cannot be reunified with their families from lingering in foster care) has found a new use in the prisons—for leveraging even relatively brief periods of incarceration into a "mandate" for the permanent removal of these children from any legal involvement with their birth parent. The heart of this act is the requirement that child welfare agencies begin the process for terminating the parent's rights if the child has been separated from a parent who is "under the state's protection for 15 of the last 22 months." A parent whose rights are terminated loses not only custody but also all of their other legal rights to the child:

rights to contact, to receive information on the child's development and well-being, to give input into important decisions in the
child's life, and to seek visits.

The Adoption and Safe Families Act drastically accelerated the
timetable under which a child welfare agency must file a petition
to terminate the rights of a parent with children in foster care, regardless of the child's age or attachment to the parent. There are
three potential exceptions to the requirement: if a relative is caring for the child in foster care, if it goes against the child's best
interests, and/or if the state has not tried to reunify the child with
his or her family. But these are rarely invoked and are seldom successful; many parents in prison barely know what is happening
and are unable to orchestrate legal representation to defend their
rights to retain access to (if not custody of) their own children.
Though some states such as Colorado have made exceptions for
incarcerated parents, many states including New York (whose
median minimum sentence is thirty-six months) have not,[10] and
others (including Vermont) fail to even recognize the act's three
exceptions.[11]

We can see the local effects of ASFA in New York State, which
operates the fourth largest state correctional system in the country.[12] Over fifty thousand men in New York's state prisons are
fathers of minor children, and the majority of the hundreds of
thousands of men who are on probation or parole or who have
cycled through New York City's jail system are parents. New York
City is home to more than 100,000 minor children with a parent
currently in prison or jail.[13] Most of those children were closely involved with their incarcerated parent prior to incarceration—over
80 percent of the mothers and 40 percent of the fathers lived with
the child prior to their arrest and incarceration.

Nationally, the implementation of ASFA has had a significant
impact on the termination of parental rights for tens of thousands
of incarcerated parents. In the five years before ASFA's enactment,
increases in incarceration rates were associated with a 67 percent

increase in termination proceedings for incarcerated parents. In the five years *after* the act was put into effect (1997–2002), despite a slowing in the rate of increase in imprisonment, parental termination proceedings increased by 108 percent.[14] In 2003 alone, over 29,000 children were removed from foster care and put up for adoption because their parents were incarcerated.[15] In 2005, 75 percent of the 2,789 women incarcerated in New York were mothers whose incarceration affected the lives of more than 5,600 children. Since the number of women incarcerated is on the rise, with the majority of incarcerated women being mothers, these statistics are unlikely to improve. Of the children placed into foster care, many are not being adopted. Between 2000 and 2004, 7,000 of the 21,000 children released for adoption in New York (33 percent) failed to be placed in a permanent home.[16]

The decision to place the child of an incarcerated woman in foster care typically means not only that a child loses a mother to prison but also that ties to a whole family unit of grandparents, siblings, and cousins are severed. By undermining the mother's morale and hope for the future, these wrenching separations further increase the likelihood of the mother's returning to prison after release. It is no surprise, then, that studies have shown that mothers are less likely to be rearrested and jailed if they are reunited with their child upon release.[17] A similar phenomenon was observed early in the HIV epidemic, where mothers who had AIDS were more likely to continue to get pregnant and give birth (often to children with a very high risk of AIDS) if they had lost their previous children to foster care or adoption.[18] For all of these reasons, the criminal justice and child welfare systems need to communicate and cooperate far better than they currently do.[19] Terminating a parent's rights to his or her children in this indiscriminate way has profound long-term effects and establishes a dangerous precedent for the systematic violation of fundamental human rights— both of the parent and of the child. One young adolescent reflects on his mother's incarceration: "I think they shouldn't have took my mama to jail that first time. Give her the opportunity to make up for what she did. Using drugs, she's hurting herself. Take her away from me, and now you're hurting me." [20]

By taking children from their imprisoned parents on a permanent basis, simply because the parents are imprisoned, we have effectively transformed parental incarceration into a mechanism for permanent family disintegration and dissolution. We are all too familiar with the history of removal of children "for their own good" in our own nation and among many native and Aboriginal societies in Canada and Australia.[21] Once again this discredited approach has been institutionalized on a large scale in the United States as a set of enforceable procedures that use parental imprisonment as an occasion for the legal termination of biological parents' rights to resume a custodial role (or even have visitation) with their own children once the parents complete a prison sentence. The persistent and highly publicized failures of child protection agencies, with their huge case loads and high staff turnover, give scant encouragement about the benefits of an increased role of these agencies in dealing with the collateral victims of mass incarceration.[22]

In the *Titanic* data, we saw that close examination of the fate of children in an epidemic or disaster can be revealing of underlying social truths. But studying a once-in-a-lifetime disaster is very different from trying to understand the implications of a mass trauma felt by millions of children and their families across decades. In the case of mass incarceration, millions of children have been and continue to be affected over an extended period of time. These effects include chronic psychological disabilities that combine with social, educational, and economic disadvantages to lead to incapacitation in these children's later lives.

The incarceration of a parent or other close family member on whom a child depends functions as a toxic exposure for that child. If this were an exposure to asbestos or radiation, we would ask questions first about its sources and severity—its prevalence—

and then seek to understand the exposure's direct and indirect consequences for children (for example, many asbestos workers' children developed lung diseases from the dust on their parents' work clothes). A national survey of prisoners' children conducted by the Bureau of Justice Statistics in 2008 found that state and federal prisons held an estimated 809,800 parents of 1,706,600 minor children. A majority of state (55 percent) and federal (63 percent) prisoners have children under the age of eighteen, and many more have adult children and grandchildren.[23]

In the United States, at the time of arrest and incarceration, 43 percent of the fathers and 64 percent of the mothers reported living with their children prior to admission to the criminal justice system. Many more had meaningful contact with their biological children despite divorce and separation—figures that are not so different from the U.S. norms. Each year hundreds of thousands of intact, two-parent households with minor children face the arrest and imprisonment of a resident parent.

Psychologist Ricardo Barreras and I developed a tool to measure the periods of children's separation from a parent due to incarceration—the most basic measure of exposure to this form of trauma. This "criminal justice calendar" is a data collection instrument designed to document each of the episodes and the total time of all these periods of parental incarceration, allowing correlation of these episodes with the child's age and other landmark events (marriage and the birth of other children, for instance) in a prisoner's life.

In a pilot study, Barreras and I interviewed eighteen formerly incarcerated parents (22 percent mothers) who together had a total of forty-nine children ages one to eighteen. We measured the timing, frequency, and duration of child-parent separation resulting from the parents' arrests and periods of imprisonment, and then calculated the children's lifetime exposure to parental incarceration.[24]

Because most adults who enter prison for the first time are

themselves very young (about 50 percent of first prison admissions are for people between eighteen and twenty-four) their children are also young—the mean age of the forty-nine children whose parents gave us data was less than six years at the time they were first separated from their parent by incarceration. The national statistics show that 10 percent of children of prisoners are born while the parent is behind bars, including the children of women who are born while the mother is in custody. (Of the children in our small sample, 20 percent were born while the parent was in prison.) Some women's prisons have nurseries that allow pregnant women in custody to deliver their children at local hospitals and then keep the children with them in prison for times varying from six months to over one year, depending on the length of sentences and expected time of release.

Reincarceration is typical, especially for drug offenders, so once a parent enters the criminal justice system, multiple separations from children becomes the norm: of the forty-nine children in our small sample, forty-three (88 percent) had at least one separation, 35 percent experienced a second separation, and 5 percent had a third separation. The length of the total time of all these separations for each child averaged 7.4 years—a figure equal to 36 percent of these children's entire lives at the time—and about half (48 percent) of all these children experienced ten or more years of separation due to incarceration by the time they were eighteen years old. As even this small group of current and former prisoners demonstrates, the children of prisoners are exposed to repeated and often long separations from their parents beginning early in their lives, when they are most vulnerable to psychological and developmental effects. It is crucial that we recognize the frequency and severity of this phenomenon for what it is—mass trauma.

From a child's perspective, parental arrest and incarceration may be seen as a special case of trauma associated with parental separation and loss—always consequential for the life of a child and for future relationships with his or her own children.

This is also true for children who lose parents in other ways—abandonment, death, war, social upheaval. Only a minute proportion of such separations (fewer than 5 percent) are from parents who are violent or abusive with their children, although even these kids often blame themselves and may prefer not to be separated, even from an abusive parent. For most of these children, the incarceration of a parent is both a wrenching loss and a source of shame and stigma—often denied or covered up by the family ("Daddy is away in the army") and not dealt with in any way that ameliorates the children's deeper reactions and confused feelings. The effects of this can be seen in the children's behavior and mental health as measured by school performance, increased incidence of psychological and behavioral problems, and increased risk of violence and future criminality on the part of the children themselves.

While these risks are readily acknowledged by all who work with such children, almost no rigorous research exists on the impact on children of parental incarceration. In part this is because of the difficulties in measuring patterns of parental involvement in the criminal justice system and calculating what this means for the lives of prisoners' children. How can exposure to parental imprisonment itself be assessed in a way that controls for the many other problems these children face, including poverty, broken families, and drugs—problems that manifest themselves in ways hard to distinguish from the effects of parental incarceration in so-called multiproblem families?[25]

The prevalence of parental incarceration is very high in those communities where recurrent arrest and incarceration are concentrated, but there is very little formally done for prisoners' children, especially by traditional child services. Indeed, the fact of their exposure to this particular trauma is often not even asked about by the many health, education, and social service agency professionals typically involved in the lives of these families. Part of this lack reflects a legitimate concern about embedding potentially stigmatizing information in a child's records. But a part also stems from a fear of opening this area to inquiry, with all of its implications for expanding the responsibilities of education, child care, and health agencies—a can of worms that most mental health and child psychology specialists are ill-prepared to address.

One vital step is to devote more attention to understanding the effects of parental incarceration on children (its prevalence and severity), in order to intervene and to reduce the damage. At a bare minimum, parental and family involvement in the criminal justice system must be acknowledged and accounted for in all of the services offered to these children and their families. Just as we need to intervene to reduce parental incarceration's immediate impacts on these children, we need to do more work to understand the role of parental incarceration as a future risk for an entire generation.

Theoretical explanatory models based on the evidence that does exist about the impact of parental incarceration on children are now beginning to emerge. Denise Johnston and Katherine Gabel have developed a model of "enduring trauma" leading to "trauma-reactive" behavior—characterized by "poor coping with losses, including disorganized and maladaptive behavior, gang membership, delinquency and early involvement in crime."[26] There is now some awareness of the cumulative effects of younger children's exposure to parental incarceration that is to be seen in teenagers who may "duplicate destructive family patterns in their own adult interpersonal lives."[27] Also, it is understood that paternal incarceration often results in serious economic crises for affected families.[28]

In response to the complex set of interconnected problems facing these families, a new conception of "fragile families" is emerging. A large Fragile Families and Child Wellbeing study is now under way as a joint program of Columbia's School of Social Work and Princeton University.[29] Research focuses on the effects of parental imprisonment on developmental outcomes for approximately three thousand urban children. Preliminary findings are that "paternal incarceration significantly increases children's externalizing problems at age five, and some evidence that [parental] incarceration increases attention problems." The study also finds that the effects of paternal incarceration "are stronger than the effects of other forms of father absence," requiring specialized support from caretakers, teachers, and social service providers. And while these effects are heightened for children who lived with their fathers prior to incarceration, they are still significant for children of nonresident fathers, "suggesting that incarceration places children at risk through family hardships including and beyond parent-child separation." [30]

Parental involvement with the criminal justice system is rarely an isolated event. More typically, it is an extended process that plays out over time and affects many family members, beginning with the immediate effects of arrest and abrupt separation from a parent. About 50 percent of the time, arrest takes place at home, within sight of the children. The next stage of this process involves repercussions from the absence of a parent while he or she is incarcerated. And finally, children must cope with the experiences associated with their parent's return from prison to the community and family.

Many more children have a father who is incarcerated than have a mother who is. Paternal incarceration appears to constitute a different set of risks for children than maternal incarceration, which more often entails risk of displacement from the home and increased likelihood of foster care or homelessness. [31] But diminished economic resources and social capital for the entire household are the norm following almost every paternal arrest and imprisonment. And often a child encounters further maternal stress, as a mother copes with spousal incarceration or that of an older child who has been contributing to family income, child care, and other household responsibilities.

Among the psychological consequences of maternal arrest and incarceration are higher rates of internalizing problems (withdrawal, frequent crying, and nightmares). By contrast, children of incarcerated fathers are more likely to exhibit acting-out problems—hostile behavior, aggression, delinquency, and school truancy. [32] These differences may be of critical significance for these children's future troubles with authorities. Thus it is crucial that we understand the consequences of our decision as a nation to imprison such a large proportion of our children's parents.

Mass incarceration in general has been described as a huge social experiment in crime control—one whose results are still poorly understood. But mass incarceration may also be seen as an even larger and less controlled experiment in the effects of the traumatic separation of millions of children from their parents. In public health, we employ long-range epidemiological studies to understand the effects of exposures to disease or toxic environments. This is the approach we are now taking to understanding the effects of mass parental incarceration upon children.

The first such large-scale prospective research program on the effects of parental incarceration on children is now under way at the Mailman School of Public Health and the Psychiatric Institute of Columbia University in New York. This study is funded by the National Institutes of Health and is being conducted in close collaboration with the Bronx Defenders, a large public defender organization that handles over twelve thousand cases each year in the Bronx Criminal Court. While stereotypes of this notoriously drug- and crime-ridden part of New York City might suggest a population of dangerous characters, in fact, over 80 percent of these cases are for nonviolent misdemeanors—most often drug offenses or minor quality-of-life offenses such as loitering or jumping a turnstile in the subway. The more violent felonies and child abuse cases (which represent less than 5 percent of all cases in the South Bronx courts) are excluded from this research. The study thus focuses specifically on the epidemic of mass incarceration, to which millions of American families have now been (and continue to be) exposed.

The research is under the direction of Dr. Christina Hoven, a child psychiatric epidemiologist whose multidisciplinary international team has studied the effects of mass trauma on children worldwide for many years, following civil wars, earthquakes, the Israel-Palestine conflict, 9/11, and the Pacific tsunami of 2004. The basis of current psychological thinking about mass trauma and its effects is the model of posttraumatic stress disorder, or PTSD.

This PTSD model for understanding the effects of mass trauma on children is now being extended to children with a history of parental incarceration, taking into account many of the factors associated with separation and loss. The research program at Columbia (in which I am an investigator) is enrolling five hundred families—half with mothers who have been arrested and half with fathers—at the point of parental arrest and arraignment in the Bronx Criminal Courts. The studies will closely follow these parents and their families for at least five years, gathering data to identify the ways in which parental arrest and incarceration impacts the children. Follow-up will include home visits, repeat interviews, and physiological measures of the children's stress responses via levels of the stress hormone cortisol. The study will also follow a control group of five hundred matched families from the same communities, where neither parent has been arrested or incarcerated during the lives of the children—a group that is proving difficult to find in the South Bronx with its high incarceration rates.

The study takes detailed family histories, including prior and current criminal justice system involvement, parental psychopathology, substance use, and poverty. Child outcomes will be monitored in two major dimensions—first, those directly related to individual child psychopathology, and second, those that might be predictive of future risk for later juvenile involvement with the criminal justice system. These outcomes are meant to inform our understanding of the transmission of high-risk behavior and elevated risk for adverse outcomes in the children of incarcerated parents. A central set of issues in this research is identifying the basis for some children's vulnerability and others' resilience with respect to issues such as drug use and violent behavior.

While we are awaiting results of these longer-term longitudinal studies, several statistical and epidemiological studies have been done that reveal a lot about what has happened to the entire population of children so heavily exposed to incarcerated parents and other family members. Sociologist Bruce Western has taken by far the most detailed look at racial and ethnic disparities associated with a history of incarceration to date (see Figure 9.1).

And demographer Christopher Wildeman has conducted a series of studies that allow us to appreciate how significant these effects are in the U.S. population. Wildeman focuses on how imprisonment transforms the life course of disadvantaged populations and how parental imprisonment alters the social experience of childhood in such a large number of African Americans that it is now visible in the vital statistics of the entire black population of the United States.[33]

Figure 9.1. Race, Education, and Imprisonment in the United States, 1980–2005

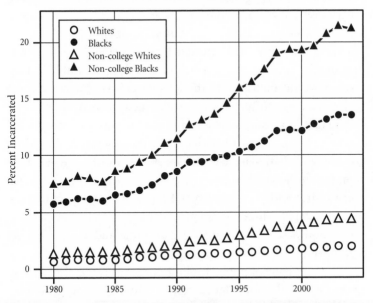

The percentage of men aged 22–30 in prison or jail shows mounting disparities by race and education between 1980 and 2005.

Source: Western, *Punishment and Inequality in America*, 17.

The extent of these effects and the form they take is truly startling. Racial inequality in parental incarceration has become far more pronounced, reflecting the dramatic growth in black incarceration rates across the decades of mass incarceration. As indicated earlier, by age fourteen, over half (50.5 percent) of all black children born in 1990 to a father who was a high school dropout had a parent imprisoned.

As imprisonment has become common for poor and minority families, and has been shown to diminish the life chances of these adults for employment, income, education, and housing,[34] incarceration exacerbates the general negative effects of all the other economic, social, ethnic, and racial inequalities evident in the United States, especially among adult men.[35] And we are now beginning to realize that it also produces broader effects during childhood and directly harms children in a number of ways previously unrecognized, including an increased likelihood of being in a gang and a shortened life expectancy.

Infant mortality rates—the death rates of children in their first year of life—are one of the benchmarks of public health and the most powerful indicator of the adverse effects of any exposure that carries risk to the still vulnerable newborn. Wildeman has, for the first time, calculated the effects of imprisonment on infant mortality rates in the United States. He uses data from the federal government's national survey of the Pregnancy Risk Assessment Monitoring System (PRAMS), a project of the Centers for Disease Control and Prevention based on detailed information provided by state health departments. PRAMS collects state-specific, population-based data on maternal attitudes and experiences before, during, and shortly after pregnancy.

A central issue of public health in America is the disparity between black and white infant mortality rates, which seems to mirror the disparity in black and white incarceration rates. According to the Department of Health and Human Services, African Americans have 2.3 times the infant mortality rate of non-Hispanic whites and are four times as likely to die as infants due to complications related to low birth weight. In addition, in 2005 African Americans had 1.8 times the sudden infant death syndrome mortality rate as non-Hispanic whites, and African American mothers were 2.5 times more likely than non-Hispanic white mothers to begin prenatal care in the third trimester, or not receive prenatal care at all.[36]

Wildeman's analysis of the parental incarceration data shows that recent parental incarceration (when controlling for other important factors including family income, employment, parental co-residence, and housing) independently affects infant mortality, elevating the risk of early infant death by 29.6 percent. This implies that, if the American imprisonment rate had remained at the 1973 level (about 120 people incarcerated for every 100,000 of the population), the entire U.S. infant mortality rate would be 5.1 percent lower today, and that the 2003 black–white inequality in infant mortality rates would be 23.3 percent lower. These dramatic results make the effects of mass incarceration upon children much more visible. They show in the starkest possible terms that mass imprisonment has disastrous consequences for both absolute levels and patterns of inequality in population health and must now be considered a major risk factor for the very survival of children.

We can estimate that 10 to 15 million minor children have by now been directly exposed to parental incarceration in the course of this thirty-five-year epidemic. With an average of about two children each for over half of all adult prison inmates, two generations of children have now had close members of their families go to prison—parents, siblings, uncles, aunts, and cousins—as well as close friends and neighbors. Today about a third of all young black men are in prison, on parole, or on probation. These are, of course, the children who came of age in the midst of the earlier period of violence and trauma of the 1980s drug wars. Growing up in the inner cities that serve as prison feeder communities—and often using and dealing drugs themselves as part of local gangs or networks that constitute the enduring legacy of drug prohibition and enforcement—these successor generations have gone on to fill juvenile detention facilities, which are often the stepping-stone to adult imprisonment.

By now we are on the third generation of these families and communities.[37] This intergenerational effect on collateral victims of adult incarceration is of a larger scale and even more damaging than the drugs themselves or the drug-related offenses that were the rationale for the arrests of so many of their parents and other family members.

Young males have always been most at risk for committing crimes and getting arrested, but in the modern era we have seen an unprecedented rise in how often that happens. In these data we can see the intergenerational effect of the war on drugs, parental incarceration, and the application of new sentencing policies, which effectively tripled the rate of incarceration for two generations of young black men as a consequence of our earlier responses to their parents' drug offenses and subsequent imprisonment (see Figure 7.4).

This pattern of multiple disadvantages implies great social and psychological vulnerability for all these families and their children.[38] Both the use of drugs and the high likelihood of prosecution of so many young adult drug users in minority communities creates a perfect storm of risks for the children exposed to parental incarceration—pushing them inexorably toward their own imprisonment by their twenties.

The confluence of these factors and the general poverty and chronic instability of those living in these communities affects almost everyone within the immediate family and those within their wider social networks. A child living in one of these feeder communities in the 1960s or 1970s had a 2–3 percent chance of having a parent go to prison; today that chance is over 30 percent. For these families, incarceration has become the norm, spawning successive generations of prison orphans and young grandmothers in their thirties and forties, now caring for the children of their imprisoned adult sons and daughters. The majority of all the extended black families and a large minority of Hispanic families (especially the poorest of them) in the United States have by now had a member incarcerated in the last thirty-five years.

These intergenerational effects of mass incarceration are clearly visible in data from the study of families that Ricardo Barreras and I did on New York's Lower East Side in 2003.[39] In this study of sixty-two families with a member recently released following a drug arrest and imprisonment, we collected family histories of drug use, arrest, and imprisonment for a total of 592 individuals: 82 percent of the families had at least one other member with a history of drug use and arrest (an average of 2.3 additional family members), 62 percent had two or more, and 40 percent had three or more. In addition, 72 percent had at least one other member with a history of imprisonment, 45 percent had two or more, and 24 percent had three or more. Of the 105 family members who were reported to have a history of imprisonment, 88 percent involved substance use. Finally, at least one member had HIV/AIDS in 49 percent of the families, with 16 percent having two or more, and 10 percent with three or more.

Studies such as this demonstrate the extent to which many families in communities such as this one are struggling with the burdens associated with having multiple relatives involved in the criminal justice system, largely related to drug use and frequently with high rates of HIV and AIDS. These data point to an important role for family-focused interventions to ameliorate the consequences of high rates of familial drug use, HIV/AIDS, incarceration, and other forms of criminal justice involvement.

But as destructive as parental incarceration is to individual children, the damage to our society of having had several generations of children with incarcerated parents is worse. Intergenerational transmission involves increased risk for these children's own future criminal involvement and imprisonment. This is perhaps the single most frightening aspect of this epidemic—and one of the strongest reasons for changing the policies that fuel mass incarceration. Recent studies have begun to confirm something we sensed was true long ago but couldn't prove: incarceration of parents breeds incarceration of their children.[39]

While "only" about 6–9 percent of all youth in the United States ages ten to seventeen are arrested each year, between 30 percent and 50 percent of those committed to juvenile detention centers (the more serious and recurrent youthful offenders) report having a parent who is or has been in prison.[40] Children of incarcerated parents show higher rates of gang membership and delinquency; they are more likely than other children to get arrested for drugs than their peers; and, ultimately, they are more likely to be incarcerated themselves.[41] Children who, by the time they are fourteen, have had a parent arrested and incarcerated commit double the average number of violent offenses by the time they are eighteen.[42]

Until quite recently, detailed examination of intergenerational consequences of mass incarceration in America has been notably absent. In part this is because it is very difficult to conduct such research. The effects of imprisonment on a family and its children are hard to disentangle from all the other depredations suffered by the poor and most marginalized populations, who are so strikingly overrepresented in prisons. But that has begun to change. Todd Clear, former president of the American Society of Criminology and dean of Rutgers School of Criminal Justice, recently published *Imprisoning Communities*, a book that captures the most basic reality of the data on the urban concentration effects of mass incarceration.[43] The concept that an entire community is adversely affected by high local imprisonment rates cuts against the common belief that this policy is somehow protective of the community—especially the notion that mass incarceration prevents crime. And it serves as the basis for understanding the research done by Clear and Rose in Florida presented earlier—that high rates of incarceration actually foster increases in crime because of the damage they do to social capital and family stability, the noncoercive mechanisms of social control that usually prevent crime in communities.

Large prison populations lead to large numbers of children with parents in prison. The actual mechanisms of transmission from one generation to the next, which make mass incarceration truly self-perpetuating, are indirect but powerful. As researchers such as Harvard sociologist Bruce Western have begun to document, incarceration disadvantages entire families economically, socially, and in other ways that preclude the children of incarcerated parents from leading productive, lawful lives.

Western summarizes the situation as follows: "When incarceration rates are high and concentrated, and incarceration has large and enduring effects on inequality (invisible, cumulative, and inter-generational) . . . mass incarceration [produces] a new social group, separated from full membership in society."[44] Western's research focuses on the major effects of imprisonment on the basic building blocks and most significant landmarks of the normal life course (education, jobs, marriage) and pinpoints the stunning disparities that so powerfully disadvantage prisoners and ex-prisoners, the vast majority of whom in our country today are African Americans.

Western produced this chart (Figure 9.2), which correlates the racial and ethnic disparity in odds of imprisonment with other landmark events (marriage, college graduation, military service).

Figure 9.2. Imprisonment and the Life Course

	Whites	Blacks
Marriage	68%	47%
Bachelor's Degree	34%	17%
Military Service	10%	9%
Imprisonment	5%	27%

Percentages of white and black men born in 1975–1979 experiencing some key life events by the time they were thirty to thirty-five years old.

Source: Bruce Western, *Punishment and Inequality in America* (New York: Russell Sage Foundation, 2006).

Higher rates of incarceration are strongly associated with lower rates of other vital events and achievements that alter the probability of success and a normal adult life course after imprisonment ends. Western examined the differences between white and black men (with their high risk of imprisonment) born between 1975 and 1979, with respect to a set of foundational life events by the year 2009, when they would be in their mid-thirties. The white/black comparisons were as follows: marriage, 68 percent vs. 47 percent; bachelor's degree, 34 percent vs. 17 percent; imprisonment, 5 percent vs. 27 percent. (Interestingly, military service was close to parity—10 percent vs. 9 percent—because the military, now engaged in several wars, can no longer afford to bar those with criminal records). The fact that racial disparities in incarceration are so closely linked to significant life outcomes only underscores the impact of mass incarceration on the life prospects of those most heavily exposed to it in America.

Western's research strikingly documents the ways in which mass incarceration has come to reproduce and sustain itself intergenerationally. Any phenomenon that so clearly and grossly impedes the life chances of a generation of parents is, by extension, going to impede the life chances of that generation's children. Epidemic mass incarceration has become one of the most powerful determinants of systematic and intergenerational inequality in our society.

10

ENDING MASS INCARCERATION: A PUBLIC HEALTH MODEL

It is not enough merely to document a great plague; the epidemiological approach must help us find ways to fight it. That is the real challenge and ultimate test of the public health paradigm and of its application to mass incarceration in America. We can now identify the features of an infectious disease gone out of control—not drug use itself, but how we handle America's drug problems. Our decision to criminalize drug use in the United States has caused our epidemic of incarceration; hence reform of our drug policies must be the first focus of our preventive strategy. But the application of a public health model of prevention also offers the prospect of a more comprehensive approach to limiting the effects of much of the damage that has already been done.

Bringing a public health approach to bear on the question of how to end the epidemic of mass incarceration and heal the damages also offers a new way to think about how to move forward in dealing with our nation's drug problems. If the goal of clinical medicine is to treat and cure individual cases of disease, in public health the primary task is always prevention. Before modern medicine had any of its current diagnostic and therapeutic expertise or the scientific means for understanding the biological basis of illness, we relied almost entirely on a well-developed public health model for the prevention of illness.

Most of what we could do to save lives back then was environmental—good sanitation and waste disposal, nutritious food, and clean water. Other effective interventions were organizational and behavioral, including having doctors wash their hands and isolating infectious individuals. The history of tuberculosis reflects the capabilities of public health in that earlier time. TB, the "white plague," was the scourge of the increasingly urbanized societies of the eighteenth and nineteenth centuries, spread by the squalor of crowded industrial cities. But TB also convincingly demonstrated the power of public health to save lives: deaths from TB in the United States and Europe were reduced by 90 percent between the late nineteenth century and 1950 by the public health interventions of isolating cases and environmental improvements such as reducing crowding and better ventilating apartments. All of that gain occurred before there was any effective medicine to treat TB; streptomycin, the first "wonder drug" that effectively cured TB, became widely available only after World War II.

Prevention of disease and its aftermath is not a simple affair. The trajectory of many diseases is complex and plays out over a long period. The clinical course of illness often involves a series of stages of the disease process, each of which requires special care—for example, an early acute phase, a dormant (often infectious) phase, and a chronic phase that may last for a lifetime. Accordingly, the public health model of prevention is comprised of three vital elements: primary, secondary, and tertiary prevention, each designed to deal with many types of illnesses and their natural stages.

Primary prevention—the prevention of new cases of the disease—is the most obvious step. If we prevent the case from occurring, nothing more is needed. The principal methods of primary prevention in medicine are immunization, pure food and water, a safe environment free of toxins, and protection from exposure to infection. Primary prevention also includes the reduction of harmful behavior (e.g., cigarette smoking) and harm reduction measures that make even dangerous behavior safer (automobile seat belts, bike helmets, safety glasses at work, clean needles for drug injectors). But we can't always succeed at primary prevention, and even if we prevent most cases, we usually don't get them all—so we need a second line of defense.

When a case of any disease has already occurred, we turn to medical care, a form of *secondary prevention*, for treatment of the individual patient. The public health model acknowledges that some people will inevitably contract the disease. Public health therefore involves medical care that tries to cure the disease or diminish the severity of symptoms. (In the case of some infectious diseases, such as TB, syphilis, and AIDS, effective medical treatment of existing cases also supports primary prevention—stopping or reducing the transmission of infection by suppressing the virus or bacteria to a low enough level that it can't easily pass from one person to another.)

Even then, some cases still may not be prevented or cured—so the final phase of the public health model seeks to limit the burden of chronic illnesses, such as diabetes or heart disease, and minimize the suffering they can cause for individuals and families. This is *tertiary prevention.* Often this works by lifetime support with medication (for example, for reducing the damages of diabetes or hypertension, or keeping HIV in check). Eyeglasses, hearing aids, wheelchairs, prostheses, and changes to the environment (including making venues accessible to the disabled) are all common forms of tertiary prevention that can make life easier for the permanently handicapped.

This public health prevention model has a direct application to the epidemic of mass incarceration. Each of the three elements of the public health model of prevention plays an important role both in minimizing the incidence of new cases of incarceration and in reducing the many unintended harms that the present structure of the criminal justice system imposes on offenders and their families. Prevention, of course, should also be designed to limit the system's contagion effects, the epidemic's ability to perpetuate itself—for example, by reducing the likelihood that a parent's arrest will increase the chances of his or her children's being arrested or imprisoned as well.

The first job for the primary prevention of mass incarceration is to reduce the number of new cases of individuals sent to prison. Secondary prevention aims to ensure that those who are now in prison are not severely or permanently incapacitated by it—that they are treated humanely, get needed medical and mental health services, and have opportunities to use the time in custody to improve the prospects of their own and their families' lives after prison, most crucially through educational programs. The last stage, tertiary prevention, applies to all the millions who have spent a large portion of their adult lives behind bars over the last three decades—most of whom are back in the community. The task of tertiary prevention is to minimize the long-term physical, mental, and social consequences that former prisoners face in the outside world. For those who have been exposed to long periods of incarceration and its aftermath of incapacitation, stigma, and disadvantage, our public health methods must help find a way for them to live productive lives in their communities and avoid re-incarceration. Some of this will entail individual help, including good medical and mental health care or drug treatment. And all will need significant assistance with housing, jobs, income support, and family relationships—not the systematic barriers now in place.

To employ a public health model of prevention we must also think beyond the usual clinical model of care that is premised on "fixing what is broken" in the individual case. In the public health approach we need to consider each part of the epidemiological triad—not just the host—by reducing exposure to the harsh punishment of imprisonment. This means altering the environment to be more protective of the most vulnerable inmates (the young), promoting healing, supporting rehabilitation, and offering proven programs to prevent relapse and recidivism. As we move toward a public health approach to criminal justice, we must do more than merely recognize the transgressions of the individual convicted of a drug offense; we must also take full societal responsibility for the collateral effects of our mass incarceration policies. This requires that we honestly address our society's own transgressions in creating such a damaging system in the first place and take steps to end the maintenance of our enormous and overly punitive criminal justice system. We must also be prepared to acknowledge and effectively deal with our criminal justice system's racial disparities, its many other injustices, and the enduring wounds it has imposed not only on prisoners but also on their families and down through the generations to their children and grandchildren.

Each of these three elements of prevention can play an important role in minimizing both the incidence of incarceration and its harms, by reducing the size of the problem (shrinking the prison population), minimizing the unwarranted incapacitation that the criminal justice system imposes on ex-offenders, addressing the collateral damages our current system causes to prisoners' families and communities, and, finally, making amends for a criminal justice system that has become a plague of prisons.

Primary Prevention

While there will always be offenders and the need to imprison some of them for public safety, the first goal in containing the epidemic of mass incarceration is to reduce the vast scale of the current criminal justice system. If high rates of imprisonment cause more harm than good, we want to prevent as many new cases of imprisonment as possible—a goal that is wholly consistent with crime prevention and public safety. We can easily identify the most preventable cases—the ones that carry least risk to the community—especially the incarceration of nonviolent drug offenders (e.g., the millions arrested for marijuana). By stopping the imprisonment of these offenders we can immediately lower the incidence of new prison entrants by about 30 percent.

Those arrested for these crimes are mostly young men who, once initiated to imprisonment, tend to cycle in and out of the system for years. So the effects of preventing a single case may have a multiplier effect over time, eliminating or reducing the recurrent cycle of reentry and recidivism that, because of sentencing policies that increase prison time for repeat offenders, drives so much of the overall size of the incarcerated population.

In the case of the U.S. epidemic, the most obvious tool for preventing mass incarceration is addressing the system of drug laws that accounts for the creation of so many new cases. The preventive measures to accomplish this are by now well recognized. They include drug law reform, the abolition of harsh mandatory sentences, and setting some broad limits on the use of incarceration as a response to drug use and addiction. A second and equally important tool is to change policing methods and enforcement practices to raise the threshold for arrest and imprisonment, creating incentives to law enforcement and the courts for the *prevention of imprisonment*, not just prevention of crime. This has been done successfully in other countries, including Canada, the United Kingdom, and Australia, through police training and support, and in the United States, on a smaller scale, through alternatives to incarceration, including social programs, drug treatment, education, and job training. We need to modify prosecutorial strategies and formally instate sentencing reforms to replace mechanistic mandatory sentences for drugs, with individual adjudication based on the facts of each case, and with a clear view to preventing the most damaging collateral effects of law enforcement and sentencing practices for the individuals and for their families.

We also need to increase the transparency and accountability of policing and modernize the strategies for law enforcement, with the goal of reining in corrupt police and overly aggressive prosecutors. We must install new incentives for deflecting young offenders from the criminal justice system altogether and engage all the system's professionals and stakeholders—police, prosecutors, the judiciary, and probation/parole departments—in the creation of new tools for the restoration of good faith with the communities they serve.

Further, the operative paradigm must be shifted to reframe the problem as one of high *incarceration* rates, not solely *crime* rates. Once we set the goal of lowering the size of the prison population (instead of locking up as many individuals as possible), our perspective on related issues will shift dramatically. Our notions of what works to reduce imprisonment will draw us to new ideas and methods to achieve public safety and security.

REDUCING THE SIZE OF THE PRISON POPULATION

Primary prevention of the epidemic of mass incarceration involves shrinking the prison system by releasing many of the people already incarcerated, preventing recidivism, and reducing the number of new cases—all without compromising public safety. In a criminal justice system as large as ours has become, this type of task will inevitably meet strong resistance from the prison-industrial complex—recall that one person is employed by the criminal justice system for every person behind bars. "Crime control" is an industry with significant economic and political clout.[1]

Yet the momentum may be shifting, and we may now have seen the apogee of the modern epidemic of mass incarceration in America. In 2009, for the first time in the thirty-five years of this epidemic of mass incarceration, the number of people behind bars actually retreated to a smaller number than the previous year. At the time I started work on this book in 2004, 2.2 million people were in prison and jail in the United States. By 2008, the number had reached 2.5 million. In 2009, however, according to a report from the Pew Center on the States based on federal statistics, while federal prison and jail populations continued to grow, the state prison system shrank for the first time in nearly forty years. Overall, the number of state prisoners in the United States may now be on the decline. As of January 1, 2010, there were 1,404,053 people under the jurisdiction of state prison authorities, 4,777 fewer than on December 31, 2008. Perhaps more significant than this small decline in the state prison populations of the country (less than 0.3 percent), the prison count dropped in twenty-six states, and some individual states have decreased the number of people incarcerated by as much as 20 percent.[2] If the pendulum has begun to swing back, as appears to be the case (using state prisons as a marker), we may say that the epidemic curve of imprisonment has begun to inflect downward—with its reproductive rate, R, now equal to less than 1. If this trend holds, we need to understand where it is coming from and to ask what we can do to sustain it.

Is the incarceration epidemic receding? Has mass incarceration reached its peak in the United States? Is the pendulum of punishment swinging back? The jury is still out on this all-important question. It is hard to derive much comfort from what may be a temporary, financially induced decrease in the number of prisoners. And because the motives for the downturn in prison populations are not completely clear, because arrest rates are still up, and because existing prison populations are still so bloated, we are assured of decades of re-entry of the damaged products of the current prison epidemic.

It may be that the thirty-five-year streak of unbroken growth in mass incarceration, fueled by prosecution of low-level drug and quality-of-life offenses, has finally reached some limit and is now entering a period of remission. But the most immediate reason for this change is clearly financial not philosophical: shortfalls in state budgets associated with the recession that began in 2008. Thus we should view the reduction in prison populations with some caution. The prison-industrial complex (a large economy in its own right) will no doubt continue to fight to sustain itself. According to the 2009 Pew study, in the midst of the decline of the larger U.S. economy, criminal correction spending was still "outpacing budget growth in education, transportation and public assistance." In 2008, two in every thirty-one adults, or 7.3 million Americans, were under the supervision of the criminal justice system—in prison, on parole, or on probation—at a cost to the states of $47 billion (this reflects a quadrupling over the past two decades; only Medicaid spending grew faster). But, when (if) the economy rebounds, vested interest groups will undoubtedly fight to restore the mass incarceration ethos that has provided a living in law enforcement and the corrections industry for so many Americans for so long. It is proving very difficult to close prisons even where population declines have emptied them.[3]

Beyond the prison lobby, old myths about the positive roles of prison die hard, especially the belief that it was mass incarceration that led to the crime drop that occurred between 1993 and 2005. The perception that mass incarceration drives down crime, self-serving as it is for the criminal justice industry that has grown so under its aegis, is very hard to dispel in public opinion. Brian Walsh, a senior research fellow at the Heritage Foundation, notes that "focusing on probation and parole could reduce recidivism and keep crime rates low in the long run," but he continues to argue that "tougher penalties for crimes . . . [drove] the crime rate down in the first place."[4]

So reduced spending on incarceration may be more indicative of hard economic times than of a fundamental shift to a less punitive approach to drug enforcement. And the shift in spending within tight budgets to less costly forms of criminal justice programs—jails instead of prisons, mandated drug treatment instead of incarceration, for instance—may prove to be short-lived. In flusher times, states have shown a preference for a highly punitive response to drug infractions, even though it is far cheaper to monitor convicts in community programs, including probation and parole. A *New York Times* survey found that thirty-four states "spent an average of $29,000 a year on prisoners, compared with $1,250 on probationers and $2,750 on parolees."[5]

Finally, putting aside future policy, we are still in a situation where millions of Americans are incarcerated because of several decades of highly punitive laws for relatively minor crimes. Overall, two-thirds of offenders, or about 5.1 million people in 2008, were on probation or parole. So while the prior period of growth of prison populations may be coming to an end, the size of the population under supervision by the criminal justice system will not shrink significantly anytime soon. Even with the decline in 2009, more than 600,000 new commitments began prison sentences that year, and over 700,000 were released and returned to the community—mostly on parole.[6]

If prison rates were restored to pre-1970s levels of 100–150 people incarcerated per 100,000 in population, this would still mean an additional 5–10 million new cases passing through the system over the next ten or twenty years, hardly a number to be proud of. These cases would of course be in addition to those of the 5 to 6 million ex-convicts who have already been through the criminal justice system and suffered its disabling effects on their lives in the outside world once released from prison. Given the current economy and the ensuing fight for social resources, there is little basis for optimism that the experiences and prospects of ex-prisoners in the coming decade will be more productive or therapeutic than the experiences of those coming out of prison over the past thirty-five years.

DRUG-SENTENCING POLICY REFORM

New York State's ultrapunitive Rockefeller drug laws helped mark the beginning of a national movement toward mandatory sentencing practices. But New York State has recently shown very promising signs of drug law reform, a key form of primary prevention of mass incarceration. After more than a decade of well-organized "Drop the Rock" efforts by individuals and advocacy groups, in 2009 the New York State government passed legislation including meaningful reform of the Rockefeller drug laws. The new changes provide judges with much greater discretion when sentencing drug offenders within certain classes and, in principle at least, will increase the use of treatment-based alternatives to incarceration.

In 2004, 2005, and 2007, some modest reforms to the Rockefeller drug laws affected a few hundred inmates. But the changes of law in 2009 saw the first significant movement toward reduction in the use of mandatory incarceration for many nonviolent drug felonies in New York State. Along with a parallel movement toward expanded treatment alternatives for drug users (besides expanded use of drug courts), these reforms are now offering the state's first intentional loosening of the punitive grip of the criminal justice system regarding drug offenses. These reforms are significant on a number of levels. Insofar as the Rockefeller drug laws are emblematic of a particularly pernicious approach to sentencing that has over the last thirty-five years spread to many states, reforms under way in New York State may provide an example for other jurisdictions considering similar changes.

A New York Legal Aid Society report found that even the modest 2004 and 2005 Rockefeller drug law reforms were a "huge success," with "tens of millions of dollars saved with low levels of recidivism by individuals released from prisons."[7] The first evaluation of the equally modest 2007 changes was also very favorable, and helps confirm the idea that reduced levels of imprisonment are not wedded to increased crime.[8]

New York prosecutors pushed back against these first sets of reforms, making what later proved to be false claims in an effort to undermine sensible, effective changes in sentencing practices. But new data emerged to counter their misleading claims. The study of the 2007 reforms showed that people who were resentenced and released early from prison had an overall recidivism rate of 8.5 percent, compared to nearly 40 percent for all others released in the same period. The report further found that New York's judges are now exercising their discretion on a case-by-case basis without compromising public safety, as evidenced by the fact that the three-year recidivism rate is about three times better than that produced by other reentry programs. "The process by which judges exercise discretion over who should be re-sentenced has shown to be effective," said William Gibney, a Legal Aid attorney and co-author of the report, who goes on to note, "Despite the claims of dangerous consequences by District Attorneys in opposing re-sentencing petitions, the people released so far under the drug law re-sentencing provisions have proven to pose a low risk to the community."

The principal sentencing reforms in New York State went into effect in October 2009, affecting a large class of nonviolent drug felonies (perhaps ten thousand cases a year) that formerly carried long mandatory prison sentences.[9] According to a June 2010 Division of Criminal Justice Services progress report, these new laws produced an immediate 28 percent drop in drug-related commitments to New York state prisons in the six months after the reforms took effect, with a reduction of fourteen hundred commitments in the first year following the reforms. In October 2010, New York State Chief Judge Jonathan Lippman announced the establishment of a Permanent Sentencing Commission "charged with conducting a comprehensive and ongoing evaluation of sentencing laws and practices and recommending reforms to improve the quality and effectiveness of statewide sentencing policy."[10] This marks an important step in the return of judicial influence on sentencing processes in New York and hopefully will lead to similar steps in other states.

These gains in prison downsizing via sentencing reform in New York State were not easy to achieve; it has taken over three decades of active opposition to the drug laws to bring about any kind of meaningful change. But we now see growing interest in modifications of some of the worst laws and sentencing practices involving specific drugs, with rescission of some of the harshest and most racially disparate crack laws under federal sentencing mandates.

Downscaling Prisons, an important report released in June 2010 by researchers at Justice Strategies and the Sentencing Project, describes a set of specific sentencing reforms and drug enforcement policies that have been implemented in four states between 1999 and 2009 and have already produced significant reductions in prison populations in these states. These four states have achieved the following declines in prison populations within the last ten years:

- New York: a 20 percent reduction, from 72,899 to 58,456, between 1999 and 2009
- New Jersey: a 19 percent reduction, from 31,493 to 25,436, between 1999 and 2009
- Michigan: a 12 percent reduction, from 51,577 to 45,478, between 2006 and 2009
- Kansas: a 5 percent reduction, from 9,132 to 8,644, between 2003 and 2009.[11]

The report attributes these declines to active political engagement, advocacy, and lobbying aimed at state legislators, and a set of new goals and "conscious efforts to change policies and practices" and reduce prison populations through sentencing and drug law reforms. These successes have many lessons for other states grappling with the effects of the economic downturn. But, as the report's authors, Judy Greene and Marc Mauer, note, there is more to it than money:

> Even prior to the onset of the latest fiscal crisis, though, legislators in many states had become increasingly interested in adopting evidence-based policies directed at producing more effective public safety outcomes. In contrast to the "get tough" climate that had dominated criminal justice policy development for many years, this new political environment has focused on issues such as diversion of people charged with lower-level drug offenses, developing graduated sanctions for people on probation and parole who break the rules, and enhancing reentry strategies.[12]

What is especially important about these states' examples is that they demonstrate the possibility of making inroads in the previously unstoppable epidemic of mass imprisonment. In most states the contagion effects of this epidemic drove U.S. imprisonment rates to record highs that only began to level off in 2009, the first year of decline in the prison population since 1973. The total reduction for these four states alone is almost 30,000 prisoners over the last decade, with a saving of about $1 billion per year in direct prison costs. The cuts also represent the prevention of about 150,000 years of life lost to imprisonment since 1999, along with all of the collateral social and economic costs this prevents.

Adding to the significance of these four states' reductions is the fact that they occurred at the same time as the total number of people being incarcerated in the rest of the nation's state prisons continued to rise—by 12 percent (from 1.17 to 1.32 million) in the ten-year period 1999–2009. Some states expanded their prison populations by more than 40 percent: West Virginia (57 percent), Minnesota (51 percent), Arizona (49 percent), Kentucky (45 percent), Florida (44 percent), and Indiana (41 percent).

While the actual reforms in the four states that enacted them were driven by years of active advocacy work in each state, the most obvious argument for extending them elsewhere is now financial: shrinking state budgets, especially following the economic crash of 2008. While most of the reductions in the four states discussed in the *Downscaling Prisons* report occurred prior to that date, we can see them as a model that other states may now emulate. States rather than the federal government bear the brunt of paying for prisons, and almost all now have or face serious deficits—with some now imposing fees on inmates to recoup the costs of their incarceration.[13] The share of state funds being spent on criminal justice costs has grown, while huge deficits loom for all the other vital functions of state and local government. But decisions to downsize the prison population based on cost-cutting imperatives, not any larger intention to reform the criminal justice system, may still achieve the desired effect of reversing the epidemic.

We have seen some signs of a backlash from some prosecutors, whose budgets and staffs increased 300 percent over the course of the war on drugs. Prosecutors' opposition to reforming New York State's Rockefeller drug laws, for example, played a critical role in delaying these changes, despite decades of evidence of their perverse effects. Many powerful prosecutors stand more than ready to publicize any failures of reform in order to "prove" that we need to keep drug offenders behind bars longer. During the presidential election of 1988, when Willie Horton was released from prison under parole reform efforts put in place by then-governor of Massachusetts Michael Dukakis, and Horton then went on to commit violent crimes, the attack campaign strategy that helped cost Dukakis the election became a model for the "soft on crime" vs. "tough on crime" discourse.

Unfortunately, many of those released under cost-cutting mandates (as in California) are being sent out of prison with even less than the typically inadequate support for reentry. And the current economic situation promises little in the way of supplementary financial resources for much-needed community services, especially education, drug treatment, jobs, housing support, and mental health care, all of which are cost-effective approaches that reduce recidivism. This could be a formula for disaster of another sort, one that may involve political exploitation of the inevitable "failures" of the trend toward deincarceration, visible in the current California clash between the state's $20 billion budget shortfall and a bloated prison system with arguably the most powerful industry lobby in the United States. (The prison industry's influence goes well beyond prison issues—for example, the California state corrections officers union played a key role in defeating a 2008 gay marriage measure.)

Secondary Prevention

For those who are already "cases" (now in prison or recently reentered and on parole or probation), secondary prevention involves reducing the direct harms and collateral consequences of incarceration and reentry. Complementing the positive effects of reducing the number of people in prison, "harm reduction" can be accomplished through modernizing the systems of policing, detention, and pretrial custody. These forms of acute exposure to the criminal justice system affect far more people (14 million arrests per year) than does long-term incarceration, and account for much destabilization of already fragile families, which often paves the way for subsequent, longer-term imprisonment.

We need to invest in more humane forms of pretrial detention and get smarter about the conditions of even brief custody, keeping young first offenders apart from older cases, putting a stop to the punitive use of isolation, and providing better protection against violence and rape. Many of the harms of prison can be addressed by better prison health services and a rehabilitative approach to imprisonment, including social and family services, educational programs, competent psychological treatment, and better connections to family and community as individuals approach reentry. All of these measures become more feasible and affordable as prisons grow smaller. (Michael Jacobson's 2005 book *Downsizing Prisons* offers a good discussion of this topic.)[14] All of these changes must be predicated on a desire to reform the punitive sentencing policies that have produced so much harsh punishment for low-level, nonviolent offenses, especially those involving drugs.

The process of secondary prevention of mass incarceration includes a series of critical interventions all along the trajectory of the criminal justice system—arrest by the police, detention, legal proceedings, sentencing, time served in prison—where intervention can counteract new "outbreaks" of the epidemic. For effective secondary prevention there is a crucial role for public advocacy in loosening the grip of our prohibitionist drug policies, and a great need to recognize the importance of fighting the legal battles that challenge these injust laws, police and prosecutorial excesses, corrupt sentencing practices, and inhumane conditions that continue to characterize mass imprisonment in the United States today.

These steps are the specific elements of a campaign of secondary prevention whose goal is to minimize the harms of current drug laws and policies, even as we struggle to change them. The individuals and organizations who work to stop this epidemic of mass incarceration and mitigate its worst effects are heroic figures fighting this epidemic on the ground and should become models of a kind of secondary prevention that citizens must practice across the nation.

PLAGUE FIGHTERS OF TULIA

Any plan for minimizing outbreaks of incarceration requires a great deal of hands-on work—there is no vaccine or magic bullet—with many stages of intervention needed. In Tulia, Texas, for example, the outbreak was ultimately reversed, although not before great harm was done to many individuals and their families. The events in Tulia and the response of advocates who fought back allow us to examine effective methods for addressing the types of outbreaks that are characteristic of harsh drug laws and the epidemic of incarceration. Tulia demonstrates how overzealous prosecutors operate around drug enforcement, where the usual standards of lawful prosecution seem not to apply. These prosecutors and task forces function like Typhoid Mary, spreading imprisonment indiscriminately. So it is appropriate to call those who identify and expose them "plague fighters."

In Tulia, a young attorney named Vanita Gupta working at the time for the NAACP Legal Defense and Educational Fund (the organization that litigated *Brown v. Board of Education* and ended the legal basis for school segregation in America) joined forces with local defense attorney Jeff Blackburn from nearby Amarillo, who worked tirelessly with a small local group—first to get the Tulia defendants out of prison and then to get their names cleared.

This would take over three years, during which more than forty Tulia residents spent time in prison. The battle of Tulia finally gained national recognition due to the inspired work of Randy Credico, a former Las Vegas stand-up comic who had worked for the human and civil rights defense attorney William Kunstler and then for the Kunstler Family Foundation. Credico went to Texas and began collaborating with the local defense committee and Blackburn, and then with the NAACP and Gupta.

The national press began to pay attention to the case, with Bob Herbert of the *New York Times* writing withering exposés about the staggering injustices of the ongoing case. Ultimately, Kunstler's daughters, who are filmmakers, documented the whole story and aired their film on national public television. These steps toward reform are the essence of preventive interventions, averting the loss of thousands of years of life that would have resulted from this single outbreak of unjust mass imprisonment.

COMMUNITY SOLIDARITY IN GREAT BARRINGTON

In Great Barrington the pushback against the large-scale police entrapment of young marijuana users came from local parents and friends of the kids whose arrest and prosecution seemed so wrong to many local citizens. Peter Greer, a former Bear Stearns hedge fund manager who had moved to Great Barrington from New York City five years earlier, had high-school-age kids and had previously been very active in Rockefeller drug law reform. Greer had lent a helping hand to a number of individual Rockefeller-era prisoners and their families who had been unfairly imprisoned in various phony drug busts and setups. He and a retired business-man, Steve Picheny, were enraged by the Great Barrington arrests and prosecutions and helped to lead a campaign to get District Attorney Capeless to back down.

When Capeless refused to talk to them about softening his ap-proach, the community group, which expanded to include many of the families of the fourteen kids who had been entrapped by the undercover agent, mounted a large public campaign, with newspaper ads and billboards across the street from Capeless's office. These were aimed both at publicizing the case—framing it in terms of unfair legal practices (rather than as a story about kids and drugs)—and at discrediting Capeless even as the campaign defended the kids. Local news stories appeared, along with letters to the editor. Others joined in a Citizens Committee for Appropriate Justice; some prominent local attorneys and businesspeople in town organized a petition drive that collected 4,000 signatures, representing half the population of the south end of the county. And as the cases moved to trial, the committee arranged to bring in Albany, New York, district attorney David Soares, who advised the group on strategy.

Soares had recently been elected after running against his then-boss, the previous Albany district attorney, who reveled in his own volume of drug prosecutions. Soares ran on a platform highlighting the futility of the Rockefeller drug laws and their disparate application in the poorest black communities of Albany. He won despite vicious opposition from the entrenched Democratic party and went on to develop many alternative programs to the Rockefeller laws for his own constituency.

Taking a lesson from Soares's success in Albany, the Great Barrington group built support for a reform-minded candidate to oppose Capeless in his upcoming bid for reelection as district attorney. Judy Knight, a Stockbridge attorney and former assistant district attorney in the Boston area, ran on an anti-drug-laws ticket and got 43 percent of the vote. But Capeless won and went on to continue hounding these kids, although the public outcry led to most of the cases being settled without prison time. Nevertheless, the prosecutions left many of the teenagers with permanent records and deep scars. But the community was now alerted to the lack of fit between the all-too-real drug problems that kids actually face and the counterproductive approach of such heavy-handed prosecution campaigns. Ironically, in the year following this "outbreak" in Great Barrington, Massachusetts passed a referendum decriminalizing possession of the small quantities of marijuana that Capeless had built his case around. The lesson here is that if local communities push back against these practices by local prosecutors, they can have an impact on the measures adopted to keep their kids safe from drugs.

HAND-TO-HAND COMBAT: LOCAL HEROES FIGHTING MASS INCARCERATION AND ITS DAMAGES

Other successful secondary prevention efforts have focused on conditions in prisons and jails. Tina Reynolds spent many years in New York state prisons on Rockefeller drug charges but is now a social worker and the head of a prisoners' rights advocacy organization, Women on the Rise Telling Her Story (WORTH). Tina organized a successful campaign against "shackling"—the practice of chaining inmates to their gurneys when they were taken outside the jail or prison to hospitals for emergency medical care. This rule was applied to pregnant women about to give birth—a ham-handed application of a general policy, and one that everyone denounced. But Tina, along with other women who had been in prison themselves, succeeded in getting New York's governor David Patterson to sign off on an executive order ending the practice in 2009.

Tina and others like her are the product of an important process by which professionally driven advocacy organizations spawn citizen activists from among the ranks of the formerly incarcerated. Many of the most effective of these have been supported by the Soros Foundation and its Open Society Institute Social Justice Fellowship Program (as I have been). Tina is also a protégé of Lynn Paltrow, the founder and executive director of National Advocates for Pregnant Women, which has worked for almost twenty years on many court cases challenging the criminal prosecution and punishment of pregnant women who have used drugs and been arrested for "giving drugs to a minor" or under child protection statutes that define the fetus in terms of anti-abortion ideology.

Often these women were arrested while seeking help for their drug problem in order to continue their pregnancies to term.

Another example of a different approach that has successfully rebuilt lives affected by drug incarceration can be found in the experience of Howard Josepher, a former heroin addict who has built and now heads Exponents/ARRIVE in New York City, a large AIDS and drug treatment program. Uniquely, this program includes teaching clients about political activism for drug law reform via their direct involvement in political advocacy. A cornerstone of ARRIVE's treatment of drug users fresh out of prisons involves organizing them to play a role in lobbying for the drug law reform that has now finally been achieved in New York State. (Talk about self-help!)

Ethan Nadelmann and Gabriel Sayegh of the Drug Policy Alliance, the leading drug reform advocacy organization in the United States, have organized many of the most successful efforts around changing the nation's drug laws—playing a central role in legal defense and in the many state campaigns for medical marijuana. Over the course of three governors' administrations in New York State, they have worked with other groups to organize campaigns and public events and hearings in New York City and Albany to confront state officials with the need to repeal the Rockefeller drug laws, often bringing in celebrities such as hip-hop mogul Russell Simmons and record company executive Jason Flom to help raise the profile of opposition to the drug laws. Other individuals and advocacy organizations in New York who have worked tirelessly to reform the Rockefeller laws include Joanne Page and Glenn Martin at the Fortune Society, Robert Gangi and Tamar Kraft-Stolar at the Correctional Association of New York, Elizabeth Gaynes at the Osborne Association—which has led the fight for a Bill of Rights for the children of incarcerated parents—and the staff of the Women's Prison Association.[15] I was present at a City College forum on youth in Harlem when Angela Jones, a young activist at the New York Civil Liberties Union, first told the story of a young man named Anthony (see chapter 7) to an audience that had no idea that New York's school safety programs had become part of the "school-to-prison pipeline." Each of these efforts is now part of a growing movement to build awareness of the vital issue of over-incarceration and needlessly harsh tactics in a world that damages so many kids in the name of protecting them from drugs. These organizations and individuals on the front lines of fighting this epidemic are all heroes—and their efforts are finally beginning to pay off.

SHIFTING THE PARADIGM

Many will say that these efforts are too modest for something as fundamental as rethinking our attitudes and policies about crime and punishment. But it is useful to recall parallels to the attitudes we once held toward another perceived threat—that of the prolif-eration of nuclear weapons during the Cold War. Not so long ago nuclear weapons were seen by most people as protection against the threat of attack by the Soviet Union or China. We can now see in retrospect how public attitudes about these weapons could change dramatically as a result of the efforts of a small (at first) but persistent public education and advocacy campaign. These efforts succeeded exactly because they were able to reframe the problem as the weapons themselves, rather than the question of national defense. The work of International Physicians for the Prevention of Nuclear War in developing and gaining publicity for a public health perspective (the threat of nuclear winter and global disas-ter) played a key role in the campaigns that successfully shifted the paradigm of how the average person viewed these weapons (and earned the group the Nobel Peace Prize in 1985). This new para-digm portrayed the weapons as a modern hazard more danger-ous than the enemies these weapons were designed to protect us from. With this new paradigm's different ways of understanding and communicating the unintended (and previously unthinkable) collateral consequences of weapons of mass destruction, the imperative for action shifted 180 degrees. Rather than wanting more and bigger bombs, the new goal became reducing these weapons to a minimum and eventually abolishing them altogether—an evolution that is now at the heart of President Obama's nuclear policies.

As the body of evidence grows about the harmful effects of mass incarceration, a similar paradigm shift is needed in our thinking about imprisonment—a paradigm shift that is (like the new view of nuclear weapons) also of great importance to our national well-being and collective security. This is the most pressing task for the final phase of the public health prevention model as applied to mass incarceration: shifting the paradigm of drug policies to produce durable changes to our society's attitudes about the use (and overuse) of arrest, criminal prosecution, and punishment by incarceration to deal with America's persistent appetite for drugs.

Tertiary Prevention

The final set of tools that public health has to offer in fighting the plague of prisons involves minimizing the suffering and disability of former prisoners, the chronic cases, to improve both the length of life and its quality for those who cannot be cured. Addressing and ameliorating the harms done to those who have suffered from our harsh drug sentencing policies over the last three decades is the hardest preventive task of all.

To begin with, the number of individuals involved is massive: an estimated 8 million to 10 million people and their families have been subjected to the toxic effects of jail or imprisonment over the course of the thirty-five-year epidemic of mass incarceration, many millions of them for drugs and related nonviolent, victimless crimes.[16] For them and their families, tertiary prevention involves dealing with the enduring stigma of prison and the burden of persistent social and economic disadvantage that is imposed by having a felony record. The task of tertiary prevention involves addressing all the adverse effects of this cumulative and long-term incapacitation and the increased risk of failure that now follows ex-prisoners back to their community and family life. The social capital these individuals have lost needs to be restored by opening the way to employment, the right to vote, and access to education and housing opportunities—the basics of a viable life outside of prison.

But tertiary prevention of mass incarceration must be approached with a sense of humility—the realization that there is also a great task of healing to be done on both sides of the equation of crime and punishment. There is a need to recognize the new opportunities both for the offender who wishes to rejoin society as a functioning adult and for the society that has heedlessly imposed so much pain and damage on those it has imprisoned for minor offenses, with all the collateral damage to innocents. As has been done in the wake of other large-scale social catastrophes such as civil wars, we must put in place a program of restorative justice, directed not just at the individuals and families caught up in mass incarceration but also at developing and employing many of the new models of crime control such as specialized community courts (mental health, drugs, housing, veterans) and the range of innovative approaches they offer.

Even with the watershed election of our first black president, *New York Times* writer Charles Blow notes that many African Americans are now living a tale of two Americas, "one of the ascension of the first black president with the cultural capital that accrues; the other of a collapsing quality of life and amplified racial tensions." Much of this collapse and related tensions among the large proportion of the population left behind has been stoked by three decades of mass incarceration of American blacks. As law professor Michelle Alexander points out in her book *The New Jim Crow*, the number of adult African Americans under the criminal justice system's control (behind bars, on parole, or on probation) now stands at 4.5 million—a figure greater than the number of adult slaves held in the United States at the start of the Civil War.[17]

To recover from a national trauma of this magnitude, we

need a new type of process that can restore the trust and good faith of all Americans who have lived through the age of mass incarceration—a collective response that must be negotiated, fashioned, and implemented with great care and transparency. The social and family networks of ex-prisoners—those who need to repair the damage done to them—have a special role to play. I believe that this country needs a formal peace process to undo the harms of the war on drugs and the effects of mass incarceration.

The most strikingly original and potentially powerful technique of restorative justice is a truth and reconciliation process of the sort that has played a crucial role in South Africa at the end of apartheid and during the peaceful transition of power in that country. South Africa's Truth and Reconciliation Commission, chaired by Archbishop Desmond Tutu, held public sessions from 1996 to 1998 and concluded its work in early 2004. The success to date of this nonviolent solution to great social injustice suggests that it is possible to achieve national resolution of a great crime against humanity without a bloodbath. This experience provides a new model of how to rebuild a damaged society without retribution, and how to deal effectively with a history of extreme violence and massive injustice. While not all parties were fully satisfied by the process, it apparently has played a crucial role in moving the society beyond the vengeance that would have destroyed the young state.

Consider the case of genocide in Rwanda, where an unprecedented level of violence and bloodshed was followed by efforts at reconciliation, the other striking case for the possibilities of restorative justice models. Today these efforts seem to be gaining traction in rebuilding that severely wounded society. Philip Gourevitch wrote about this process in the *New Yorker*:

In the course of a hundred days, beginning on April 6, 1994, nearly a million people from the Tutsi minority were massacred in the name of an ideology known as Hutu Power. On the fifteenth anniversary of the genocide, Rwanda is one of the safest and most orderly countries in Africa. The great majority of prisoners accused or convicted of genocide have been released. And Rwanda is the only nation where hundreds of thousands of people who took part in mass murder live intermingled at every level of society with the families of their victims. "So far, so good," Rwanda's President Paul Kagame tells the writer.[18]

The case of mass incarceration in the United States must be next. At the start of the second decade of the twenty-first century, America needs to devise a plan of restorative justice as part of its recovery from the damages of more than three decades of mass incarceration. The country must design and begin to build programs that utilize these same types of models and employ national and local truth and reconciliation processes that begin to undo the harms of mass incarceration in many communities. These forums need to acknowledge publicly the damage done by the excesses of mass incarceration and see its millions of victims as the casualties of a long civil war. The massive injustice of this war's racial dimensions and its disparities represent a huge burden imposed on the already most disadvantaged minority communities, especially African Americans. This is one of our own society's greatest crimes against the humanity of millions of our countrymen, and it must now spur a call to action.

The restorative justice model plan must include a vital role for local churches and community-based organizations, especially those organizations that already work with prisoners and their families.[19] A body of restorative justice models has grown out of work in Native American communities based on models of "healing circles," building upon traditional tribal conflict-resolution methods. Several restorative justice organizations already exist across America and are well positioned to take on the vital task of designing and implementing community-based truth and reconciliation dialogues and forums, where local law enforcement and the community at large can open a conversation with those who have served time in prisons and with their families. These forums need to document the impact of both crime and mass incarceration on these communities' social capital.

The problem of mass incarceration is now clear, and its resolution is enormously important to our nation's future. There has been too much damage and loss already, and there is blame enough to go around. We should no longer need to justify the sort of reconciliation processes that can undo the most egregious effects of these past thirty-five years of mass incarceration. It is time to begin to restore the vast amounts of social capital and goodwill that have been lost. Specific measures should include an amnesty from the effects of a criminal record on individuals who have completed their sentences, with assurances for the prospect of a full life that minimizes the harms done to their children and future generations.

Moving from the current failed model of retributive justice to a model based on rebuilding social capital and restorative justice would be the most radical paradigm shift of all. In the case of epidemic mass incarceration, this will involve more than tinkering with the rules or even amending bad laws and fighting their unjust applications (although that is vital). To approach this stage of prevention we must think about larger issues and new ideas about crime and punishment. We must develop new models and methods for our criminal justice system that value the lives and dignity of all of our people—even those who transgress. These new models must allow room for the triumph of social justice over the increasingly punitive society that mass incarceration has spawned in America. If we can achieve this goal, we will have come full circle in our efforts at prevention, where our efforts to limit the harms of mass incarceration come to be practiced as primary prevention to end this age of mass incarceration and help immunize us against any future plague of prisons in America.

NOTES

1. An Epidemiological Riddle

1. http://www.eyewitnesstohistory.com/pftitanic.htm.

2. Cholera in London: The Ghost Maps of Dr. Snow

1. From William Blake's poem "Jerusalem" (1804), http://www.progres
   siveliving.org/william_blake_poetry_jerusalem.htm. When Blake
   wrote these words England was still a largely rural place, a "green and
   pleasant land." However, the Industrial Revolution was already well
   under way; factories had sprung up and the old cottage industries
   were disappearing, soon replaced by new industries and the concentration of the population into crowded cities that became incubators
   for many diseases.
2. Sir John Simon, *Report on the Last Two Cholera-Epidemics of London
   as Affected by the Consumption of Impure Water; Addressed to the Rt.
   Hon. the President of the General Board of Health, by the Medical Officer of the Board. Presented to Both Houses of Parliament by Command
   of Her Majesty* (London: Eyre and Spottiswoode, 1856), 18, available
   at http://collections.nlm.nih.gov/pageturner/viewer.html?PID=nlm:
   nlmuid-0260772-bk; John Snow, *On the Mode of Communication
   of Cholera* (London: John Churchill, 1855). For epidemiology, see
   http://www.ph.ucla.edu/epi/snow/snowbook.html.
3. Steven Johnson, *The Ghost Map: The Story of London's Most Terrifying
   Epidemic and How It Changed Science, Cities, and the Modern World*
   (New York: Riverhead, 2007).

4. Centers for Disease Control and Prevention, *Principles of Epidemiology in Public Health Practice*, 3rd ed. (Washington, DC: Department of Health and Human Services, 2007).

5. P. De Kruif, *Microbe Hunters* (New York: Harcourt, 2002).

6. Snow, *On the Mode of Communication of Cholera.*

7. Johnson, *Ghost Map.*

3. AIDS: The Epidemiology of a New Disease

1. "Pneumocystis Pneumonia—Los Angeles," *Morbidity and Mortality Weekly Report* 30 (1981): 250–52.

2. "First Reports of AIDS and Growth of Epidemic," *Morbidity and Mortality Weekly Report* 50, no. 21 (2001).

3. Charles F. Turner et al., *AIDS: Sexual Behavior and Intravenous Drug Use* (Washington, DC: National Academy Press, 1989).

4. *Advancing HIV Prevention: New Strategies for a Changing Epidemic* (Atlanta: Centers for Disease Control and Prevention, 2007).

5. William W. Darrow, "AIDS: Socio-epidemiological Response to an Epidemic," in *AIDS and the Social Sciences*, ed. Richard Ulack and William Francis Skinner (Lexington: University of Kentucky Press, 1991).

6. Randy Shilts, *And the Band Played On: Politics, People, and the AIDS Epidemic* (New York: St. Martin's Press, 1987).

7. Paul A. Volberding, Merle A. Sande, Joep Lange, and Warner C. Greene, eds., *Global HIV/AIDS Medicine* (Philadelphia: Saunders/Elsevier, 2007).

8. Fears about how AIDS was transmitted exaggerated the dangers of heterosexual transmission and everyday contact; see Michael Crichton, "Panic in the Sheets," *Playboy*, December 1991; and Joseph Berger, "Communion-Cup Fear Addressed," *New York Times*, September 13, 1985. "In 1985, at 13, Ryan White became a symbol of the intolerance that is inflicted on AIDS victims. Once it became known that White, a hemophiliac, had contracted the disease from a tainted blood transfusion, school officials banned him from classes" ("American Notes: Voices: The Miracle of Ryan White," *Time*, April 23, 1990).

9. Volberding et al., *Global HIV/AIDS Medicine*; Turner et al., *AIDS.*

10. Volberding et al., *Global HIV/AIDS Medicine.*

11. Françoise Barre-Sinoussi et al., "Isolation of a T-Lymphotropic Retrovirus from a Patient at Risk for Acquired Immune Deficiency Syndrome (AIDS)," *Science*, May 20, 1983.

12. Robert Pear, "AIDS Blood Test to Be Available in 2 to 6 Weeks," *New York Times*, March 3, 1985; J.L. Marx, "A Virus by Any Other Name?" *Science*, March 22, 1985.

13. UN AIDS Data, http://www.unaids.org/en/KnowledgeCentre/HIV Data/default.asp.

14. Ernest Drucker and Sten H. Vermund, "Estimating Population Prevalence of Human Immunodeficiency Virus Infection in Urban Areas with High Rates of Intravenous Drug Use: A Model of the Bronx in 1988," *American Journal of Epidemiology* 130, no. 1 (July 1989).

15. "Epidemiologic Notes and Reports: Possible Transfusion-Associated Acquired Immune Deficiency Syndrome, AIDS—California," *Morbidity and Mortality Weekly Report*, December 10, 1982, 652–54.

16. Jonathan Mann, Daniel Tarantola, and Thomas Netter, *AIDS in the World* (Cambridge, MA: Harvard University Press, 1992).

17. P.A. Selwyn, D. Hartel, W. Wasserman, and E. Drucker, "Impact of the AIDS Epidemic on Morbidity and Mortality Among Intravenous Drug Users in a New York City Methadone Maintenance Program," *American Journal of Public Health* 79, no. 10 (1989): 1358–63; Ernest Drucker, "AIDS and Addiction in New York City," *American Journal of Drug and Alcohol Abuse* 12, no. 1–2 (1986): 165–81.

18. Gerald H. Friedland, Brian R. Saltzman, Martha F. Rogers, Patricia A. Kahl, Martin L. Lesser, Marguerite M. Mayers, and Robert S. Klein, "Lack of Transmission of HTLV-III/LAV Infection to Household Contacts of Patients with AIDS or AIDS-Related Complex with Oral Candidiasis," *New England Journal of Medicine* 314, no. 6 (February 6, 1986): 334–49.

19. Peter A. Selwyn, *Surviving the Fall: The Personal Journey of an AIDS Doctor* (New Haven, CT: Yale University Press, 1998).

20. UN AIDS data.

21. Rodrick Wallace, "Traveling Waves of HIV Infection on a Low Dimensional 'Socio-Geographic' Network," *Social Science and Medicine* 32, no. 7 (1991): 847–52.

22. Diana M. Hartel, Ellie E. Schoenbaum, Peter A. Selwyn, Gerald H. Friedland, Robert S. Klein, and Ernest Drucker, "Patterns of Heroin, Cocaine and Speedball Injection Among Bronx (USA) Methadone Maintenance Patients: 1978–1988," *Addiction Research & Theory* 3, no. 4 (1996): 323–40; Ernest Drucker, Cristian Apetrei, Robert Heimer, and Preston Marx, "The Role of Unsterile Injections in the HIV Pandemic," in Volberding et al., *Global HIV/AIDS Medicine.*

23. William J. Sabol, Heather C. West, and Matthew Copper, "Prisoners in 2008," Bureau of Justice Statistics, revised June 30, 2010, http://bjs.ojp.usdoj.gov/content/pub/pdf/p08.pdf; Ryan S. King and Marc Mauer, "Distorted Priorities: Drug Offenders in State Prisons," The Sentencing Project, Washington, DC, September 2002.

24. Anne C. Spaulding, Ryan M. Seals, Matthew J. Page, Amanda K. Brzozowski, William Rhodes, and Theodore M. Hammett, "HIV/AIDS Among Inmates of and Releasees from US Correctional Facilities, 2006: Declining Share of Epidemic but Persistent Public Health Opportunity," *PLoS ONE* 4, no. 11 (2009): e7558.

4. A Different Kind of Epidemic

1. The Sentencing Project, "New Incarceration Figures: Thirty-Three Consecutive Years of Growth," December 2006, http://www.sentencingproject.org/doc/publications/inc_newfigures.pdf.

2. Lauren E. Glaze and Laura M. Maruschak, "Parents in Prison and Their Minor Children," NCJ222984, U.S. Department of Justice, Bureau of Justice Statistics, January 2009, 2, http://www.ojp.usdoj.gov/bjs/pub/pdf/pptmc.pdf.

3. William J. Sabol and Heather Couture, "Prison Inmates at Midyear 2007," NCJ221944, U.S. Department of Justice, Bureau of Justice Statistics, June 2008, http://www.ojp.usdoj.gov/bjs/pub/pdf/pim07.pdf.

4. Todd Clear, *Imprisoning Communities: How Mass Incarceration Makes Disadvantaged Neighborhoods Worse* (New York: Oxford University Press, 2007).

5. Bruce Western, *Punishment and Inequality in America* (New York: Russell Sage Foundation, 2006).

6. Ibid.; Christopher Wildeman, "Parental Imprisonment, the Prison Boom, and the Concentration of Childhood Disadvantage," *Demography* 46, no. 2 (2009): 265–80.

7. The total public expenditures on the criminal justice system (police, courts, and corrections) from 1982 to 2010 was $3.7 trillion. Bureau of Justice Statistics, "Direct Expenditures by Criminal Justice Function, 1982–2006," U.S. Department of Justice, http://bjs.ojp.usdoj.gov/content/glance/tables/exptyptab.cfm.

8. William J. Sabol, Heather C. West, and Matthew Cooper, "Prisoners in 2008," Bureau of Justice Statistics, NCJ 228417, December 2009 (revised June 30, 2010), http://bjs.ojp.usdoj.gov/content/pub/pdf/

p08.pdf; Todd Minton, "Jail Inmates at Midyear 2009," Bureau of Justice Statistics Statistical Tables, NCJ 230122, June 2010, http://bjs.ojp .usdoj.gov/content/pub/pdf/jim09st.pdf.

9. C. Puzzanchera, B. Adams, and W. Kang, "Easy Access to FBI Arrest Statistics: 1994–2007," Office of Justice Programs, U.S. Department of Justice, http://www.ojjdp.ncjrs.gov/ojstatbb/ezaucr/asp/ucr_ display.asp.

10. Bureau of Justice Statistics, Federal Criminal Case Processing, 2000, with Trends 1982–2000," U.S. Department of Justice, November 2001, p. 12, Table 6, http://bjs.ojp.usdoj.gov/content/pub/pdf/fccp00.pdf

11. Ibid.; William J. Sabol, Heather C. West, and Matthew Cooper, "Prisoners in 2008," Bureau of Justice Statistics, revised June 30, 2010, http://bjs.ojp.usdoj.gov/content/pub/pdf/p08.pdf.

12. "World Prison Brief—Highest to Lowest Figures," International Centre for Prison Studies, School of Law, King's College London, http:// www.kcl.ac.uk/depsta/law/research/icps/worldbrief/wpb_stats.php.

13. Bureau of Justice Statistics, "Total Correctional Population," U.S. Department of Justice, http://bjs.ojp.usdoj.gov/index.cfm?ty=tp&tid=11.

14. Marc Mauer, "The Changing Racial Dynamics of the War on Drugs," The Sentencing Project, Washington, DC, 2009; Michael H. Tonry, *Malign Neglect: Race, Crime, and Punishment in America* (New York: Oxford University Press, 1995); Katherine Beckett, Kris Nyrop, and Lori Pfingst, "Race, Drugs, and Policing: Understanding Disparities in Drug Delivery Arrests," *Criminology* 44, no. 1 (February 2006): 105–38.

15. American Correctional Association, *A 21st Century Workforce for America's Correctional Profession* (Alexandria, VA: American Correctional Association, 2004).

16. "California Proposition 5 (2008)," Ballotpedia, http://ballotpedia .org/wiki/index.php/California_Proposition_5_%282008%29.

17. Judith Greene and Marc Mauer, *Downscaling Prisons: Lessons from Four States* (Washington, DC: The Sentencing Project, 2010); Harry G. Levine and Deborah Peterson Small, *The Marijuana Arrest Crusade: Racial Bias and Police Policy in New York City, 1997–2007* (New York: New York Civil Liberties Union, 2008), http://www.nyclu.org/ files/MARIJUANA-ARREST-CRUSADE_Final.pdf.

18. Clear, *Imprisoning Communities.*

19. Shannon McCaffrey, "Aging Inmates Clogging Nation's Prisons," Associated Press, September 30, 2007; Ronald H. Aday, *Aging Prisoners: Crisis in American Corrections* (New York: Praeger, 2003).

5. Anatomy of an Outbreak:
New York's Rockefeller Drug Laws and the Prison Pump

1. Malcolm M. Feeley and Sam Kamin, "The Effect of 'Three Strikes and You're Out' on the Courts: Looking Back to See the Future," in *Three Strikes and You're Out: Vengeance as Public Policy*, ed. David Shichor and Dale K. Sechrest (Thousand Oaks, CA: Sage, 1996), 137–39.
2. H. Irene Hall et al., "Estimation of HIV Incidence in the United States," *JAMA* 300, no. 5 (August 6, 2008): 520–29.
3. New York State Department of Corrections Criminal Justice Performance Management, "2009 Criminal Justice Crimestat Report," June 30, 2010, http://criminaljustice.state.ny.us/pio/annualreport/2009 -crimestat-report.pdf.
4. William J. Sabol, Heather C. West, and Matthew Cooper, "Prisoners in 2008," Bureau of Justice Statistics, revised June 30, 2010, http://bjs .ojp.usdoj.gov/content/pub/pdf/p08.pdf.
5. Unpublished data, Bronx Defenders.
6. Ibid.

6. Orders of Magnitude:
The Relative Impact of Mass Incarceration

1. Office of Vital Statistics, "Summary of Vital Statistics: 2008," New York City Department of Health and Mental Hygiene, http://www .nyc.gov/htm/doh/downloads/pdf/vs/2008sum; for AIDS data, see HIV Epidemiology and Field Services, "New York City HIV/AIDS Annual Surveillance Statistics," New York City Department of Health and Mental Hygiene, http://www.nyc.gov/html/doh/html/ah/hiv tables.shtml.
2. Tyler McCormick, Matthew J. Salganik, and Tian Zheng, "How Many People Do You Know? Efficiently Estimating Personal Network Size," *Journal of the American Statistical Association* 105, no. 489 (2010): 59–70.

7. A Self-Sustaining Epidemic: Modes of Reproduction

1. Alfred Blumstein, Jacqueline Cohen, Jeffrey A. Roth, and Christy A. Visher, eds., *Criminal Careers and "Career Criminals," Volume I* (Washington, DC: National Academy Press, 1986).

2. Katherine Gabel and Denise Johnston, *Children of Incarcerated Parents* (New York: Lexington Books, 1995).

3. Ernest Drucker, "Mass Incarceration in America," in *The State of Black America 2003*, ed. Lee A. Daniels (New York: National Urban League, 2003).

4. Robert Perkinson, *Texas Tough: The Rise of America's Prison Empire* (New York: Metropolitan Books, 2010); Texas Department of Criminal Justice, "Annual Report 2008," http://www.tdcj.state.tx.us/mediasvc/annualreview2008.pdf.

5. Scott Henson, "Slash the Prison Population," *Texas Monthly*, May 2009.

6. Scott Henson, "Texas Incarceration Far Outstrips Population Growth," Grits for Breakfast, January 25, 2007, http://gritsforbreakfast.blogspot.com/2007/01/texas-incarceration-far-outstrips.html.

7. William Finnegan, "Deep East Texas," *New Yorker*, August 22, 1994, 72.

8. Bob Herbert, "Partway to Freedom," *New York Times*, June 16, 2003; "Transcript: Truth and Lies," *NOW*, PBS, August 22, 2003, http://www.pbs.org/now/transcript/transcript_tulia.html.

9. Ibid.; Andrew Gumbel, "An American Travesty," *The Independent*, August 20, 2002.

10. Bob Herbert, "A Good Day," *New York Times*, June 16, 2003.

11. Ray Rivera, Al Baker, and Janet Roberts, "A Few Blocks, 4 Years, 52,000 Police Stops," *New York Times*, July 12, 2010.

12. Harry G. Levine and Deborah Peterson Small, *The Marijuana Arrest Crusade: Racial Bias and Police Policy in New York City, 1997–2007* (New York: New York Civil Liberties Union, 2008), http://www.nyclu.org/files/MARIJUANA-ARREST-CRUSADE_Final.pdf, 5; Harry G. Levine, "New York City's Marijuana Arrest Crusade . . . Continues," September 2009, http://dragon.soc.qc.cuny.edu/Staff/levine/NYC-MARIJUANA-ARREST-CRUSADE-CONTINUES-FEB-2010.pdf.

13. Harry G. Levine and Loren Siegel, "$75 Million a Year: The Cost of New York City's Marijuana Possession Arrests," Drug Policy Alliance, March 15, 2011, http://www.drugpolicy.org/resource/75-million-year-cost-new-york-citys-marijuana-possession-arrests.

14. Alice Speri, "2010 Marijuana Arrests Top 1978–96 Total," City Room Blog, NYTimes.com, February 11, 2001, http://cityroom.blogs.nytimes.com/2011/02/11/marijuana-arrests-increase-in-new-york-city/.

15. Ibid.; Levine and Small, *Marijuana Arrest Crusade*.

16. Drug Policy Alliance, "2010 NYC Marijuana Arrest Numbers Released: 50,383 New Yorkers Arrested for Possessing Small Amounts of Mari-

juana," press release, February 10, 2011, http://www.drugpolicy.org/news/2011/02/2010-nyc-marijuana-arrest-numbers-released-50383-new-yorkers-arrested-possessing-small-; John Del Signore, "Welcome to NYC, 'Marijuana Arrest Capital of the World,'" Gothamist, February 10, 2011, http://gothamist.com/2011/02/10/welcome_to_nyc_the_marijuana_arrest.php.

17. Harry G. Levine, Jon B. Gettman, Loren Siegel, and the Marijuana Arrest Research Project, *Targeting Blacks for Marijuana: Possession Arrests of African Americans in California, 2004–08* (Los Angeles, CA: Drug Policy Alliance, 2010), http://www.drugpolicy.org/docUploads/Targeting_Blacks_for_Marijuana_06_29_10.pdf

18. Division of Criminal Justice Services, Office of Justice Research and Performance, "2009 Drug Law Reform Preliminary Update on Early Implementation," New York State Department of Corrections, February 2010, http://criminaljustice.state.ny.us/drug-law-reform/documents/drug-law-reform-presentation-feb2010.pdf.

19. Glenn C. Loury, *Race, Incarceration, and American Values* (Cambridge, MA: MIT Press, 2008), 8.

20. Ibid., 7.

21. Ricardo Barreras, "Minor Charges, Serious Consequences: The Collateral Damage of Misdemeanor Arrest," report, Open Society Institute/Bronx Defenders, forthcoming.

22. New York Civil Liberties Union, "School to Prison Pipeline," http://www.nyclu.org/issues/youth-and-student-rights/school-prison-pipeline.

23. Jeremy Travis, *But They All Come Back: Facing the Challenges of Prisoner Reentry* (Washington, DC: Urban Institute Press, 2005).

24. Michelle Alexander, *The New Jim Crow: Mass Incarceration in the Age of Colorblindness* (New York: The New Press, 2010).

25. Mindy Brittner, student project at Barnard College, 2007–8, based on U.S. Census data and Bureau of Justice Statistics annual prison surveys.

26. U.S. Sentencing Commission, "U.S. Sentencing Commission Promulgates Permanent Amendment to the Federal Sentencing Guidelines Covering Crack Cocaine, Other Drug Trafficking Offenses," press release, April 6, 2011, http://www.ussc.gov/Legislative_and_Public_Affairs/Newsroom/Press_Releases/20110406_Press_Release.pdf.

27. Ernest Drucker, ed. "The Crack Chronicles: Perspectives on Understanding the Trajectory of a New Drug," special issue editor and introduction, *Addiction Research and Theory* 11, no. 1 (February 2003).

28. James Bonta and D.A. Andrews, *Risk-Need-Responsivity Model for Offender Assessment and Rehabilitation* (Ottawa: Public Safety Canada, 2007), available at http://www.publicsafety.gc.ca/res/cor/rep/risk_need_200706-eng.aspx; *Beyond the Revolving Door: A New Response to Chronic Offenders: Report of the Street Crime Working Group to the Justice Review Task Force* (Victoria, BC: BC Justice Review Task Force, 2005), available at http://www.bcjusticereview.org/working_groups/street_crime/scwg_report_09_29_05.pdf.

29. New York State Department of Corrections Criminal Justice Performance Management, "2009 Criminal Justice Crimestat Report," June 30, 2010, http://criminaljustice.state.ny.us/pio/annualreport/2009-crimestat-report.pdf; Justice Mapping Center website, http://www.justicemapping.org/.

30. Ernest Drucker and Ricardo Barreras, "Assessing Children's Exposure to Parental Incarceration: An Epidemiological Approach," Abstract #111443, presented at the 2005 American Public Health Association annual meeting, Philadelphia, PA.

31. Anne Dannerbeck, "Differences Between Delinquent Youth with and Without a Parental History of Incarceration," School of Social Work, University of Missouri, Columbia, 2005, www.mjja.org/images/docs/Children%20of%20Sub%20Abusers.pdf; Nell Bernstein, "When the Jailhouse Is Far from Home: Kids with Parents Behind Bars Share the Pain of Incarceration," A Sentence of Their Own, http://www.asentenceoftheirown.com/Essays%20-%20Jailhouse.html.

32. Denise Johnston, *Children of Offenders* (Pasadena, CA: Pacific Oaks Center for Children of Incarcerated Parents, 1992); Denise Johnston, *Children of the Therapeutic Intervention Project* (Pasadena, CA: Pacific Oaks Center for Children of Incarcerated Parents, 1993).

33. Christina W. Hoven, Ernest Drucker, Cristiane S. Duarte, et al., "Stress and Justice Studies: Maternal Incarceration and Course of Child Psychopathology in the South Bronx," New York State Psychiatric Institute, 2010, http://report.nih.gov/rcdc/categories/ProjectSearch.aspx?FY=2009&ARRA=Y&DCat=Violence%20Research; Fragile Families and Child Wellbeing Studies, http://www.fragilefamilies.princeton.edu/about.asp.

34. Christopher Wildeman, "Parental Imprisonment, the Prison Boom, and the Concentration of Childhood Disadvantage," *Demography* 46, no. 1 (February 2009); Becky Pettit, "Growing Up with an Imprisoned Parent: The Implications of Mass Imprisonment for the Future of American Inequality," proposal to the Russell Sage Foundation, October 14, 2009.

35. William Julius Wilson, *When Work Disappears: The World of the New Urban Poor* (New York: Knopf, 1996); William Julius Wilson, *The Truly Disadvantaged: The Inner City, the Underclass, and Public Policy* (Chicago: University of Chicago Press, 1987).

36. Robert D. Putnam, *Bowling Alone: The Collapse and Revival of American Community* (New York: Simon & Schuster, 2000).

37. Jeffrey Fagan, Valerie West, and Jan Holland, "Reciprocal Effects of Crime and Incarceration in New York City Neighborhoods," *Fordham Urban Law Journal* 30 (2003): 1551–1602.

38. Todd R. Clear, "Backfire: When Incarceration Increases Crime," *Journal of the Oklahoma Criminal Justice Research Consortium* 3, no. 2 (1996): 1–10; Dina R. Rose and Todd R. Clear, "Incarceration, Social Capital and Crime: Examining the Unintended Consequences of Incarceration," *Criminology* 36, no. 3 (1998).

39. Craig Reinermann, "Cannabis Policies and User Practices: Market Separation, Price, Potency, and Accessibility in Amsterdam and San Francisco," *International Journal of Drug Policy*, no. 1 (January 2009): 28–37.

40. Ryan S. King and Marc Mauer, "The War on Marijuana: The Transformation of the War on Drugs in the 1990s," *Harm Reduction Journal* 3, no. 6 (2006); Levine and Small, *Marijuana Arrest Crusade.*

41. D.A. Andrews and James Bonta, *The Psychology of Criminal Conduct*, 4th ed. (Newark, NJ: Anderson, 2006).

8. Chronic Incapacitation:
The Long Tail of Mass Incarceration

1. Marc Mauer and Meda Chesney-Lind, eds., *Invisible Punishment: The Collateral Consequences of Mass Imprisonment* (New York: The New Press, 2002).

2. David Garland, *Punishment and Modern Society: A Study in Social Theory* (Chicago: University of Chicago Press, 1993).

3. Jeremy Travis, *But They All Come Back: Rethinking Prisoner Reentry* (Washington, DC: U.S. Department of Justice, Office of Justice Programs, 2000).

4. Bruce Western, *Punishment and Inequality in America* (New York: Russell Sage Foundation, 2006).

5. Steven D. Levitt and Stephen J. Dubner, *Freakonomics: A Rogue Economist Explores the Hidden Side of Everything* (New York: William Morrow, 2005).

6. Heather MacDonald, "Fighting Crime Where the Criminals Are," *New York Times*, June 25, 2010.

7. World Health Organization, "DALYs/YLDs Definition," http://www.who.int/mental_health/management/depression/daly/en.

8. Ibid.

9. See *Estelle v. Gamble*, U.S. Supreme Court, 1964.

10. Travis, *But They All Come Back*; Patrick A. Langan and David J. Levin, "Recidivism of Prisoners Released in 1994," Bureau of Justice Statistics Special Report NCJ 193427, U.S. Department of Justice, Washington, DC, June 2, 2002.

11. Robert Greifinger, ed., *Public Health Behind Bars: From Prisons to Communities* (New York: Springer, 2007).

12. "Putting Policy into Practice on Prison Health," *Lancet Infectious Diseases* 7, no. 8 (August 2007): 497.

13. Correctional Association of New York, "Healthcare in New York Prisons 2004–2007," February 2009, http://www.correctionalassociation.org/publications/download/pvp/issue_reports/Healthcare_Report_2004-07.pdf.

14. Robert B. Greifinger, "Inmates Are Public Health Sentinels," testimony before Commission on Safety and Health in U.S. Prisons, Washington, DC, June 28, 2005, http://www.prisoncommission.org/statements/greifinger_robert.pdf.

15. Women in Prison Project, "Survivors of Abuse in Prison Fact Sheet," April 2009, http://www.correctionalassociation.org/publications/download/wipp/factsheets/Survivors_of_Abuse_Fact_Sheet_2009_FINAL.pdf.

16. Diane C. Hatton and Anastasia A. Fisher, eds. *Women Prisoners and Health Justice: Perspectives, Issues, and Advocacy for an International Hidden Population* (Oxford: Radcliffe, 2009); Pamela M. Diamond et al., "The Prevalence of Mental Illness in Prison," *Administration and*

Policy in Mental Health and Mental Health Services Research 29, no. 1 (2001).

17. Allen J. Beck and Paige M. Harrison, *Sexual Victimization in Prisons and Jails Reported by Inmates, 2008–09* (Washington, DC: Bureau of Justice Statistics, 2010), available at http://bjs.ojp.usdoj.gov/con tent/pub/pdf/svpjri0809.pdf. See also Prison Rape Elimination Act of 2003, P.L. 108-79, 2003 U.S. Code, http://bjs.ojp.usdoj.gov/index .cfm?ty=tp&tid=20.

18. Devon B. Adams, Allen J. Beck, and Paige M. Harrison, "Sexual Violence Reported by Correctional Authorities, 2006," U.S. Department of Justice, Bureau of Justice Statistics, August 16, 2007, http://bjs.ojp .usdoj.gov/index.cfm?ty=pbdetail&iid=1151.

19. Jeremy Travis, "Charting a New Course: A Blueprint for Transforming Juvenile Justice in New York State," report of Governor David Paterson's Task Force on Transforming Juvenile Justice, December 2009, http://www.vera.org/download?file=2944/Charting-a-new-course-A -blueprint-for-transforming-juvenile-justice-in-New-York-State.pdf.

20. Greifinger, *Public Health Behind Bars*.

21. Ibid.

22. Ibid.

23. Christopher J. Mumola and Jennifer C. Karberg, "Drug Use and Dependence, State and Federal Prisoners, 2004," U.S. Department of Justice, Bureau of Justice Statistics, NCJ 213530, October 2006, http:// bjs.ojp.usdoj.gov/content/pub/pdf/dudsfp04.pdf.

24. United Nations Office on Drugs and Crime, "Drug Treatment and Rehabilitation in Prison Settings," http://www.unodc.org/treatment/ en/drug_treatment_in_prison_settings_references.html.

25. Ingrid A. Binswanger, Marc F. Stern, and Joann G. Elmore, "Mortality After Release from Prison," author/editor response, *New England Journal of Medicine* 356 (April 26, 2007).

26. Roy Walmsley, "World Prison Population List, Sixth Edition," King's College London, 2009, http://www.scribd.com/doc/328143/ World-Prison-Population-List-2007.

27. "Drug Treatment in the Criminal Justice System," Office of National Drug Control Policy, March 2001, http://www.whitehousedrugpol icy.gov/publications/factsht/treatment/index.html.

28. Michael Rothfeld, "State to Eliminate 40% of Funding Designed to Turn Prisoners' Lives Around," *Los Angeles Times*, October 17, 2009.

29. Kate Dolan, Wayne Hall, and Alex Wodak, "Methadone Maintenance Reduces Injecting in Prison," letter to the editor, *BMJ* 312, no. 7039 (1996): 1162.

30. Ibid.

31. Timothy W. Kinlock, Michael S. Gordon, Robert P. Schwartz, Terrence T. Fitzgerald, and Kevin E. O'Grady, "A Randomized Clinical Trial of Methadone Maintenance for Prisoners," *Journal of Substance Abuse Treatment* 37, no. 3 (2009): 277–85; Jennifer C. Karberg and Doris J. James, "Substance Dependence, Abuse, and Treatment of Jail Inmates," U.S. Department of Justice, Bureau of Justice Statistics, NCJ 209588, July 2005, http://bjs.ojp.usdoj.gov/content/pub/pdf/sdatji02 .pdf.

32. Binswanger et al., "Mortality After Release from Prison."

33. H. Irene Hall et al., "Estimation of HIV Incidence in the United States," *JAMA* 300, no. 5 (August 6, 2008): 520–29.

34. "HIV/AIDS Among Women," Centers for Disease Control and Prevention, August 2008, http://www.cdc.gov/hiv/topics/women/ resources/factsheets/women.htm.

35. Kristen Tillerson, "Explaining Racial Disparities in HIV/AIDS Incidence Among Women in the U.S.: A Systematic Review," *Statistics in Medicine* 27, no. 20 (2008): 4132–43.

36. Anne C. Spaulding, Ryan M. Seals, Matthew J. Page, Amanda K. Brzozowski, William Rhodes, and Theodore M. Hammett, "HIV/AIDS Among Inmates of and Releasees from US Correctional Facilities, 2006: Declining Share of Epidemic but Persistent Public Health Opportunity," *PLoS ONE* 4, no. 11 (2009): e7558.

37. Thomas A. Peterman, Catherine A. Lindsey, and Richard M. Selik, "This Place Is Killing Me: A Comparison of Counties Where the Incidence Rates of AIDS Increased the Most and the Least," *Journal of Infectious Diseases* 191, Suppl. 1 (2005): S123–26.

38. Adaora A. Adimora and Victor J. Schoenbach, "Social Context, Sexual Networks, and Racial Disparities in Rates of Sexually Transmitted Infections," *Journal of Infectious Diseases* 191, Suppl. 1 (2005): S115–22.

39. Bernard E. Harcourt, "Cruel and Unusual Punishment," in *Encyclopedia of the American Constitution, Supplement II*, ed. Leonard Levy, Kenneth Karst, and Adam Winkler (New York: Macmillan, 2000); Bernard E. Harcourt, "The Mentally Ill, Behind Bars," *New York Times*, January 15, 2007.

40. Christopher J. Mumola, "Suicide and Homicide in State Prisons and Local Jails," U.S. Department of Justice, Bureau of Justice Statistics, NCJ 210036, August 2005, http://bjs.ojp.usdoj.gov/content/pub/pdf/shsplj.pdf.

41. Atul Gawande, "Hellhole," *New Yorker*, March 30, 2009.

42. Jeffrey L. Metzner and Jamie Fellner, "Solitary Confinement and Mental Illness in U.S. Prisons: A Challenge for Medical Ethics," *Journal of the American Academy of Psychiatry and the Law* 38, no. 1 (2010).

43. Gawande, "Hellhole."

44. Jennifer Gonnerman, *Life on the Outside: The Prison Odyssey of Elaine Bartlett* (New York: Farrar, Straus and Giroux, 2004).

45. Bruce Western, *Punishment and Inequality in America* (New York: Russell Sage Foundation, 2006); Jeremy Travis and Michelle Waul, eds., *Prisoners Once Removed: The Impact of Incarceration and Reentry on Children, Families, and Communities* (Washington, DC: Urban Institute Press, 2003).

46. Christopher Wilderman, "Parental Imprisonment, the Prison Boom, and the Concentration of Childhood Disadvantage," *Demography* 46, no. 1 (February 2009).

47. Jeff Manza and Christopher Uggen, "The President Is Right: Ex-Felons Need Aid," *Newsday*, February 5, 2004.

48. "No Second Chance: Federal 'One Strike' Legislation," Human Rights Watch Report, 2004.

49. "Is a Convicted Felon Currently on Probation Eligible for the HUD Subsidized Housing Program?" FHA Home Mortgage Loan Interest Rates, May 22, 2009, http://fha-loanrates.com/articles/is-a-convicted-felon-currently-onprobation-eligible-for-the-hud-sub sidized-housing-program/.

50. Council of State Governments, "Homelessness Is Prevalent Among People Released from Prison and Jail," 2008, http://reentry policy.org/Report/PartII/ChapterII-D/PolicyStatement19/Research Highlight19-1.

51. Ibid.

52. S. Metraux and D. Culhane, "Homeless Shelter Use and Reincarceration Following Prison Release: Assessing the Risk," Center for Studies on Addiction, School of Social Work, University of Pennsylvania, October 2002, http://povertyandhomelessness.wikispaces.com/file/view/dennis_culhane_prison_paper.pdf.

53. Caterina Gouvis Roman and Jeremy Travis, *Taking Stock: Housing, Homelessness, and Prisoner Reentry* (Washington, DC: Urban Institute, 2004), available at http://www.urban.org/url.cfm?ID=411096.

54. "Prison > Homelessness," A Public Defender, August 17, 2007, http://apublicdefender.com/2007/08/17/prison-homelessness.

55. Thelton E. Henderson Center for Social Justice, "Barriers to Employment & Reentry for Formerly Incarcerated People," annotated bibliography, UC Berkeley School of Law, December 2008.

56. American Bar Association Commission on Effective Criminal Sanctions and the Public Defender Service for the District of Columbia, *Internal Exile: Collateral Consequences of Conviction in Federal Laws and Regulations* (Chicago: American Bar Association, 2009), http://www.abanet.org/cecs/internalexile.pdf.

57. David R. Jones, "Ex-Prisoners and Jobs," *Gotham Gazette*, May 2006, http://www.gothamgazette.com/article/socialservices/20060524/15/1862.

58. Darren Wheelock, "Collateral Consequences and Racial Inequality: Felon Status Restrictions as a System of Disadvantage," *Journal of Contemporary Criminal Justice* 21, no. 1 (2005): 82–90.

59. Henrie M. Treadwell and Elisabeth Kingsbury, "Ex-Felons Denied Foodstamps, Other Assistance," *Black Star News*, December 17, 2009.

60. Alexander Kirshner, "The International Status of the Right to Vote," Democracy Coalition Project, November 2003, http://www.demcoalition.org/pdf/International_Status_of_the_Right_to_Vote.pdf; Richard S. Katz, *Democracy and Elections* (New York: Oxford University Press, 1997), 216.

61. "The Sentencing Project Publishes Report on Disenfranchisement Reform," press release, The Sentencing Project, September 25, 2008.

62. Ibid.

9. The Contagion of Punishment: Collateral Damage to Children and Families of Prisoners

1. Bruce Western, *Punishment and Inequality in America* (New York: Russell Sage Foundation, 2006).

2. Lori B. Girshik, *Soledad Women: Wives of Prisoners Speak Out* (Westport, CT: Praeger, 1996).

3. Bruce Western, "Incarceration, Marriage and Family Life," working paper, September 2004, Russell Sage Foundation, http://www.russellsage

.org/publications/workingpapers/incarcerationmarriagefamilylife/
document.

4. Ibid., 22–23.

5. Sara McLanahan et al., *The Fragile Families and Child Wellbeing Study: Baseline National Report* (Princeton, NJ: Bendheim-Thoman Center for Research on Child Wellbeing, 2003).

6. Bendheim-Thoman Center for Research on Child Wellbeing, "Fragile Families Research Brief 12," October 2002, 3.

7. William Julius Wilson, *When Work Disappears: The World of the New Urban Poor* (New York: Knopf, 1996).

8. Dan Bloom, "Employment-Focused Programs for Ex-Prisoners: What Have We Learned, What Are We Learning, and Where Should We Go from Here?" MDRC, July 2006, http://www.mdrc.org/publications/435/full.pdf.

9. Osborne Association, *How Can I Help?*, 3 vol. pamphlet set, http://www.osborneny.org/publications.htm.

10. Patricia E. Allard and Lynn D. Lu, *Rebuilding Families, Reclaiming Lives: State Obligations to Children in Foster Care and Their Incarcerated Parents* (New York: Brennan Center for Justice at New York University School of Law, 2006), 4.

11. Maryann Zavez, "Use of the Adoption and Safe Families Act at 15/22 Months for Incarcerated Parents," *Vermont Law Review* 33, no. 2 (2008): 187–99.

12. "Prison and Jail Inmates at Midyear 2004—NCJ #," NCJ-208801, U.S. Department of Justice, Bureau of Justice Statistics, April 2005, http://bjs.ojp.usdoj.gov/content/pub/pdf/pjim04.pdf.

13. The Osborne Association is the lead convener of the New York City Initiative on Children of Parents in Prison, and is currently involved in a system-wide assessment of policies affecting children following the arrest of a parent.

14. Julie Kowitz Margolies and Tamar Kraft-Stolar, "When 'Free' Means Losing Your Mother," Women in Prison Project of the Correctional Association of New York, February 2006, xi.

15. Allard and Lu, *Rebuilding Families, Reclaiming Lives.*

16. Kowitz Margolies and Kraft-Stolar, "When 'Free' Means Losing Your Mother," 16.

17. Allard and Lu, *Rebuilding Families, Reclaiming Lives*, 5.

18. Anitra Pivnick, "Kinchart-Sociograms as a Method for Describing the Social Networks of Drug-Using Women," *NIDA Monograph 165*

(1996): 167–20:; K. Eric, E. Drucker, D. Worth, B. Chabon, A. Pivnick, and K. Cochrane, "The Women's Center: A Model Peer Support Program for High Risk IV Drug and Crack Using Women in the Bronx," *International Conference on AIDS* 5 (June 4–9, 1989): 760 (abstract no. Th.D.P.7).

19. Michelle Cornacchia, "Critical History of the Adoption and Safe Families Act," unpublished research report, New Jersey College of Medicine and Dentistry, February 2010.

20. Allard and Lu, *Rebuilding Families, Reclaiming Lives.*

21. Michael Downey, "Canada's Cultural Genocide: Forced Removal of Native Children," *Contemporary Issues Companion: Genocide*, ed. William Dudley (Detroit: Greenhaven Press, 2001); Peter Read, *The Stolen Generations: The Removal of Aboriginal Children in New South Wales 1883 to 1969* (Surry Hills, NSW: Department of Aboriginal Affairs, 2006).

22. "Interview: Martin Guggenheim," "Failure to Protect," *Frontline*, PBS, 2010, http://www.pbs.org/wgbh/pages/frontline/shows/fostercare/inside/guggenheim.html.

23. Christopher J. Mumola, "Incarcerated Parents and Their Children," U.S. Department of Justice, Bureau of Justice Statistics, NCJ 192335, August 2000, http://bjs.ojp.usdoj.gov/content/pub/pdf/ipte.pdf; Lauren E. Glaze and Laura M. Maruschak, "Parents in Prison and Their Minor Children," NCJ 2222984, Bureau of Justice Statistics, August 8, 2008, http://bjs.ojp.usdoj.gov/index.cfm?ty=pbdetail&iid=823.

24. Ricardo Barreras, Ernest Drucker, and David Rosenthal, "The Concentration of Substance Use, Criminal Justice Involvement, and HIV/AIDS in the Families of Drug Offenders," *Journal of Urban Health* 82, no. 1 (2005): 162–70.

25. Adrian Nicole LeBlanc, *Random Family: Love, Drugs, Trouble, and Coming of Age in the Bronx* (New York: Scribner, 2003).

26. Katherine Gabel and Denise Johnston, *Children of Incarcerated Parents* (New York: Lexington Books, 1995).

27. Quoted in ibid.

28. Creasie Finney Hairston, "Prisoners and Their Families: Parenting Issues During Incarceration," *From Prison to Home: The Effect of Incarceration and Reentry on Children, Families, and Communities*, U.S. Department of Health and Human Services, Assistant Secretary for Planning and Evaluation, and Substance Abuse and Mental Health Services Administration, December 2001, http://aspe.hhs.gov/hsp/prison2home02/Hairston.htm.

29. Fragile Families and Child Wellbeing Study, "Study Topics," http://www.fragilefamilies.princeton.edu/collaborative.asp.

30. Amanda Geller, Carey E. Cooper, Irwin Garfinkel, Ofira Schwartz-Soicher, and Ronald B. Mincy, "Beyond Absenteeism: Father Incarceration and Its Effects on Children's Development," working paper WP09-20-FF, Center for Research on Child Wellbeing, Woodrow Wilson School of Public and International Affairs, Princeton University, January 25, 2010.

31. Christopher Wildeman, "Parental Incarceration, Child Homelessness, and the Invisible Consequences of Mass Imprisonment," Working Paper WP09-19-FF, Center for Research on Child Wellbeing and Fragile Families, April 2010, http://crew.princeton.edu/working papers/WP09-19-FF.pdf.

32. Travis A. Fritsch and John D. Burkhead, "Behavioral Reactions of Children to Parental Absence Due to Imprisonment," *Family Relations* 30 (1982).

33. Christopher Wildeman, "Parental Imprisonment, the Prison Boom, and the Concentration of Childhood Disadvantage," *Demography* 46, no. 2 (2009): 265–80.

34. Leonard M. Lopoo and Bruce Western, "Incarceration and the Formation and Stability of Marital Unions," *Journal of Marriage and the Family* 67, no. 3 (2005): 721–34; Michael Massoglia, "Incarceration as Exposure: The Prison, Infectious Disease and Other Stress-Related Illnesses," *Journal of Health and Social Behavior* 49, no. 1 (2008): 56–71; Jason Schnittker and Andrea John, "Enduring Stigma: The Long-Term Effects of Incarceration on Health," *Journal of Health and Social Behavior* 48, no. 2 (2007): 115–30.

35. Massoglia, "Incarceration as Exposure."

36. "Infant Mortality and African Americans," U.S. Department of Health and Human Services, http://minorityhealth.hhs.gov/tem plates/content.aspx?ID=3021.

37. "School to Prison Pipeline: Fact Sheet," New York Civil Liberties Union, http://www.nyclu.org/schooltoprison.

38. Western, *Punishment and Inequality in America.*

39. Barreras, Drucker, and Rosenthal, "Concentration of Substance Use."

40. Denise Johnston, *Children of the Therapeutic Intervention Project* (Pasadena, CA: Pacific Oaks Center for Children of Incarcerated Parents, 1993).

41. Nell Bernstein, "When the Jailhouse Is Far from Home," A Sentence of Their Own, http://www.asentenceoftheirown.com/Essays%20-%20 Jailhouse.html; Anne Dannerbeck, "Differences Between Delinquent Youth with and Without a Parental History of Incarceration," School of Social Work, University of Missouri, Columbia, 2005, www.mjja .org/images/docs/Children%20of%20Sub%20Abusers.pdf; Prison Visitation Project, *Needs Assessment of Children Whose Parents Are Incarcerated* (Richmond, VA: Department of Mental Health, Mental Retardation, and Substance Abuse Services, 1993).

42. Denise Johnston, *Children of Offenders* (Pasadena, CA: Pacific Oaks Center for Children of Incarcerated Parents, 1992); Lauren E. Glaze and Laura M. Maruschak, "Parents in Prison and Their Minor Children," NCJ222984, U.S. Department of Justice, Bureau of Justice Statistics, January 2009, 2, http://www.ojp.usdoj.gov/bjs/pub/pdf/ pptmc.pdf.

43. J. David Hawkins, Todd I. Herrenkohl, David P. Farrington, Devon Brewer, Richard F. Catalano, Tracy W. Harachi, and Lynn Cothern, "Predictors of Youth Violence," *OJJDP Juvenile Justice Bulletin*, April 2000.

44. Dina R. Rose and Todd R. Clear, "Incarceration, Social Capital and Crime: Examining the Unintended Consequences of Incarceration," *Criminology* 36, no. 3 (1998); Todd R. Clear, *Imprisoning Communities: How Mass Incarceration Makes Disadvantaged Neighborhoods Worse* (New York: Oxford University Press, 2007).

45. Bruce Western, "Mass Incarceration: An Update," Columbia Population Research Center seminar, February 18, 2010.

10. Ending Mass Incarceration: A Public Health Model

1. Nils Christie, *Crime Control as Industry* (London: Routledge, 1998).

2. Pew Center on the States, "Prison Count 2010: State Population Declines for the First Time in 38 Years," issue brief, April 2010, http://www .pewcenteronthestates.org/uploadedFiles/Prison_Count_2010.pdf.

3. Ibid; "Expensive Prisons," editorial, *New York Times*, February 7, 2011.

4. Brian Walsh, "The Criminal Intent Report: Congress Must Justify New Criminalization," Heritage Foundation, June 9, 2010, http:// www.heritage.org/Research/Reports/2010/06/The-Criminal-Intent -Report-Congress-Must-Justify-New-Criminalization.

5. Jennifer Steinhauer, "To Cut Costs, States Relax Prison Policies," *New York Times*, March 24, 2009.

6. "Testimony of Jeremy Travis, President of John Jay College of Criminal Justice, Before the U.S. House of Representatives, Committee on Appropriations, Subcommittee on Commerce, Justice, Science, and Related Agencies," March 12, 2009, http://www.jjay.cuny.edu/Travis_Congressional_Testimony.pdf; Heather Couture and William J. Sabol, "Prison Inmates at Midyear 2007," Bureau of Justice Statistics, June 6, 2008, NCJ 221994, 4, http://bjs.ojp.usdoj.gov/index.cfm?ty=pbdetail&iid=840.

7. New York Legal Aid Society, "Report on Impact of Drug Law Reform," November 2009. See also "New Legal Aid Society Report Finds That 2004 and 2005 Rockefeller Drug Law Reforms Huge Success," press release, Drug Policy Alliance, January 14, 2010, http://www.drugpolicy.org/news/pressroom/pressrelease/pr011410.cfm.

8. William Gibney, personal communication.

9. 2009 Drug Law Reform Update, New York State Department of Corrections, Division of Criminal Justice Services, June 16, 2010.

10. New York State Unified Court System, "Chief Judge Announces Creation of Permanent Sentencing Commission for New York State," press release, October 13, 2010, http://www.nycourts.gov/press/pr2010_11.shtml.

11. Judith Greene and Marc Mauer, *Downscaling Prisons: Lessons from Four States* (Washington, DC: The Sentencing Project, 2010).

12. Ibid., 3.

13. Rebekah Diller, "The Hidden Costs of Florida's Criminal Justice Fees," Brennan Center for Justice, New York University School of Law, March 23, 2010, http://www.brennancenter.org/page/-/Justice/FloridaF%26F_ExecSum.pdf?nocdn=1.

14. Michael Jacobson, *Downsizing Prisons: How to Reduce Crime and End Mass Incarceration* (New York: NYU Press, 2006).

15. The Fortune Society, http://fortunesociety.org/; the Correctional Association of New York, http://www.correctionalassociation.org/; the Osborne Association, http://www.osborneny.org/; and the Women's Prison Association, http://www.wpaonline.org/.

16. Becky Pettit and Bruce Western, "Mass Imprisonment and the Life Course: Race and Class Inequality in U.S. Incarceration," *American Sociological Review* 69, no. 2 (2004): 151–69.

17. Charles M. Blow, "Black in the Age of Obama," *New York Times*, December 4, 2009; Michelle Alexander, *The New Jim Crow: Mass Incarceration in the Age of Colorblindness* (New York: The New Press, 2010).

18. Philip Gourevitch, "The Life After: Fifteen Years After the Genocide in Rwanda, the Reconciliation Defies Expectations," *New Yorker*, May 4, 2009.

19. Howard Zehr, *The Little Book of Restorative Justice* (Intercourse, PA: Good Books, 2002); Kay Pranis, "Restoring Community: The Process of Circle Sentencing," paper presented at the "Justice Without Violence: Views from Peacemaking Criminology and Restorative Justice conference, June 6, 1997, http://www.doc.state.mn.us/rj/publications/circle.htm; see also the Capital Restorative Justice project, http://www.capitalrestorativejustice.org; Community Works restorative justice models, Family Transition Circles, http://www.communityworkswest.org/index.php/rgc/52-ftc.

INDEX

Note: Figures are represented by the letter "f" following a page number.